FREEDOM
IN CHRIST

Leader's Guide

THE GRACE COURSE

An **8-Session Guide** to Experiencing

Freedom and Fruitfulness in Christ

STEVE GOSS

& Freedom in Christ Ministries

BETHANYHOUSE
a division of Baker Publishing Group
BethanyHouse.com

> WHAT LEADERS SAY ABOUT THE GRACE COURSE

"The Grace Course is a tremendous course with profound and liberating truth which every Christian can apply. It helps you to get rid of your old baggage of lies and legalism, enjoy freedom in Christ, and experience the life of Christ in abundance."

Valeriy Kudaev, Pastor, Face to Face Church, Saint Petersburg, Russia

"As someone who has studied and taught considerably about the grace of God, I was not expecting the life-changing impact that The Grace Course had on me! I experienced a deeper encounter with God's grace and love that freed me to obey Him more faithfully. Now I want to help everyone in our church to know God in this way."

Sharon Nash, Executive Director of Discipleship, Swallowfield Chapel, Kingston, Jamaica

"The Grace Course has blessed me personally by helping me understand that in Christ I am perfectly loved and accepted because of who I am in Christ, not because of what I do. It has helped my church return to its first love of God. Instead of being motivated by shame, guilt, fear or pride, people have become fruitful disciples of Jesus."

Pastor Michael Obino, Uganda Christian Fellowship Mission, Serere, Uganda

"The Grace Course is timeless. I have seen lives changed, hearts softened and biblical truths embraced as people live out and demonstrate the grace that is our inheritance from God."

Lory Matthews, IBC Biblical Counselor, Syracuse, New York, United States

"For those of us who live in the baptismal waters of Confucian culture, the true grace we learn in this course equips us to live in the freedom God has given us. "

Jiwook Huh, Senior Pastor, Mokyang Church, Seoul, Korea

"The Grace Course goes deep very quickly, and this can be uncomfortable for some, but each person who attended the course grew in their faith hugely. The Holy Spirit brought people to a place of new understanding of who they were in Christ. It was beautiful to see and a privilege to lead."

Revd. Janet May, North Creedy East Mission Community, Devon, UK

"The Freedom in Christ Course is an excellent course to discover the freedom we have in Christ and the fullness of life that is available to us in Christ. Equally excellent and transforming is The Grace Course that empowers one to live out that freedom by the truth of God's Word and the power of the Holy Spirit."

Bernie McGale, Discipleship Pastor, Rice Road Community Church, Welland, Ontario, Canada

"The Grace Course helps us understand and experience God's grace fully so that we serve Him out of love rather than out of fear, selfish ambition, or any other reason."

Shirley Ip, Global CTM, Hong Kong

"The Grace Course is phenomenal! It has helped many of our participants, including myself, to realize the lies that have kept us in fear and doubt and has empowered us with the Word of God to continually move forward in victory upon victory."

Christopher Johnson, Group Leader, Grace Fellowship Church,
Latham, New York, United States

"We would recommend this course to any church. It has given us the tools to know who we are in Christ and equip others to become fruitful disciples of Christ."

Srdjan & Ruth Vorotovic, Word of God Evangelical Church, Kotor, Montenegro

"Many know God cares and know what Jesus did for them but somehow sense that He loves others more or that there's a need to do more to get His attention and earn His love. The Grace Course will help you know His deep love for YOU. It's a real revelation that He chooses you, delights in you, and wants you to enjoy life with HIM now, just being You!"

Janice Kirkpatrick , Carnmoney Presbyterian Church,
Co Antrim, Northern Ireland

"I highly recommend The Grace Course. It teaches us about the Father's love and helps us move on from Pharisaical religion, pride, and judging others."

Pastor Isaac Opolot, Pentecostal Assemblies of God, Kamacha, Uganda

"The Grace Course opens Christians' eyes so that they really know God as their loving Father. Both young and old were moved to tears when they suddenly experienced His love in a new, deeper way and freely gave their hearts back to Him."

Reni Boss & Tobias Müller, Online Course Leaders,
IAM–Mission.de, Switzerland and Germany

"The Grace Course reaches the shaded areas of our life and character that aren't changed through normal preaching, and creates an opportunity for the Spirit of God to bring deep transformation."

Helcio & Angela Lange da Silva, Evangelical Church,
Mondim de Basto, Portugal

"Many individuals from our church, including myself, have found a new level of freedom from attending The Grace Course. It helps us understand that we are no longer orphans but have been completely restored and do not need to feel guilty or shameful anymore."

Jennifer Tosten, Christ Freedom Ministry Associate,
The Ark Fellowship, Cypress, Texas

"'Pride goes before destruction and a haughty spirit before a fall'" (Proverbs 16:18). The insight from The Grace Course on humility has been an ongoing, life-changing journey of avoiding destruction and falls for me personally and for the congregation that the Lord allows me to lead. The effect I've seen in my church has been spiritual growth and increased membership. I recommend this course because the freedom that comes with humility leaves so much room for God to be exalted."

Jamesetta Roach, Senior Pastor, The Throne Room Worship Center,
St. Louis, Missouri, United States

"We used The Grace Course with those battling addiction. They were able to identify with the son who ran away, and it promoted deep discussions on the goodness of God and their identity in Christ."

Dawn Shearsmith, FIC and Alpha Courses Leader,
Emmanuel Church, Durham, UK

"The Grace Course embraces much more than the generic understanding of 'God's unmerited favor.' It addresses head on the paralyzing false motivators of shame, guilt, fear, and pride with both the 'want to' and the 'strength to' love others unconditionally and become a fruitful follower of Jesus. It's refreshing that the course never fails to impact my life personally and my relationship with others."

Doug Sargeant, Retired pastor and Freedom in Christ facilitator, City Centre Baptist
Church, Mississauga, Ontario, Canada

"We've seen The Grace Course transform lives by helping people apply the Word of God practically. With its focus on knowing and living from our identity in Christ, many people now live free from fear and walk in God's love and joy."

Patrick and Crystal Hammond, Pastors, New Destiny
Christian Center, Kent, Washington, United States

"I had begun to distance myself from brothers in Christ, but The Grace Course gave me a fresh enthusiasm for unity. It is a great tool for churches, families, and individuals that helps us replace wrong thinking with God's truth."

Martin Emeru, Pastor, Uganda Christian Fellowship Mission, Soroti, Uganda

"The Grace Course is powerful, especially in combination with The Freedom In Christ Course. What appear to be simple Biblical truths are presented in a way that penetrates the heart and fosters the beginning of deep healing."

Mark Eshelman PhD, MDiv, Prayer Leader, Sierra Pines Church,
Oakhurst, California, United States

DEDICATION

This new version of The Grace Course is dedicated to

Paul Travis

07 March 1933–21 December 2023

Happy to be described affectionately as "our recovering legalist," Pastor Paul Travis described his journey from legalism to grace in *Grace That Breaks The Chains* (Harvest House, 2014).

Paul and his wife Joyce traveled to England and Northern Ireland to speak at conferences I organized in 2006. They were hugely significant in helping me understand grace at a much deeper level and Paul's teaching was the inspiration for The Grace Course.

He dedicated the last decades of his life to working for Freedom In Christ Ministries in the United States where he and Joyce led many into freedom.

Paul was—indeed is—a humble, teachable servant of Jesus who made a huge impact on very many, including me. I praise God for the legacy he leaves.

Steve Goss

Thanks!

I feel embarrassed that my name is the only one on the cover of this book because so many other people have made such significant contributions to the content of the course and to the process of making it happen.

The hallmark of our amazing global Freedom In Christ team is that they don't look for recognition or reward beyond knowing that they are contributing to seeing this life-changing message continue to bring transformation.

But I want to let you know who these amazing people are who gave so much time and put in so much effort to make this new version of *The Grace Course* possible. Thank you all so much.

Steve

MY CO-AUTHORS ON THE ORIGINAL GRACE COURSE

Jude Graham, a key member of Freedom In Christ's team based in Northern Ireland, was the inspiration for putting this message of grace into the form of a course. Jude made huge contributions to the original version of the course, particularly to *The Steps To Experiencing God's Grace*.

Rich Miller, former president of Freedom In Christ USA and co-author of the first edition of *The Grace Course,* has a wonderful gift for communicating God's truth. Many of his wonderful illustrations and insights endure in this new version.

THE GRACE COURSE PROJECT TEAM

Warren Jantz (Team Leader)

Sue Jantz

Sue Lindsay

Charlene Munro

Adela Apetroaie and her team of intercessors

OTHER AMAZING CONTRIBUTIONS

Jess Regnart

Tim Baynes Clarke

Vic Ford

Josué Reed Maldonado

Bex Moye

Zoe Goss

Roberto Reed

Sue Huber

Sara Hudson

Erin Casey

Jon Smethurst

Marianne Becker

THE GRACE COURSE AND WONDER OF GRACE PRESENTERS

Rob Davies

Leisha Lyn-Cook

Nancy Maldonado

Josh Shaarda

Sidhara Udalagama

TESTIMONY FILMING

Caroline Kihanda

Sami Kimita

Andrew Walkington

Hunter Starmer

Warren Jantz

Sue Jantz

Alice Osborne

Alan Osborne

Kristjan Juu

Contents

FOREWORD 10

WELCOME 11

session **01 FREE!** 31

session **02 UNASHAMED!** 47

session **03 INNOCENT!** 65

session **04 VICTORIOUS!** 79

session **05 COURAGEOUS!** 95

session **06 CALM!** 109

session **07 FRUITFUL!** 127

session **08 PEACEMAKER!** 141

THE STEPS TO EXPERIENCING GOD'S GRACE 157

STRONGHOLD-BUSTING 173

RESOURCES 189

Foreword

By *Dr. Neil T. Anderson*

Founder and President Emeritus of Freedom In Christ Ministries

A newly adopted child found himself in a big mansion. His new Father whispered in his ear, "This is yours, and you have a right to be here. I have made you a joint heir with my only begotten Son. He paid the price that set you free from your old taskmaster who was cruel and condemning. I purchased it for you because I love you." The young boy couldn't help but question this incredible gift. "This seems too good to be true. What did I do to deserve this?" he wondered. "I have been a slave all my life, and I have done nothing to earn such a privilege!"

He was deeply grateful, however, and began to explore all the rooms in the mansion. There were many other people in the mansion who also had been adopted. He began to form new relationships with his adopted brothers and sisters. He especially enjoyed the buffet table from which he freely ate. Then it happened! While turning away from the buffet table he knocked over a stack of glasses and a valuable pitcher that crashed to the floor and broke. Suddenly he began to think, "You clumsy, stupid kid! You will never get away with this. What right do you have to be here? You better hide before someone finds out because they will surely throw you out."

At first he was caught up with the wonder of living in the mansion with a whole new family and a loving Father, but now he was confused. Old tapes laid down in early childhood began to play again in his mind. He was filled with guilt and shame. The thoughts continued. "Who do you think you are? Some kind of a privileged character? You don't belong here any more, you belong in the basement!" "The old taskmaster was right about me, I don't belong here," thought the newly adopted child. So he descended into the basement of despair.

The cellar was dreary and dark. The only light came from the open door at the top of the long stairs. He heard his Father calling for him, but he was too ashamed to answer. He was surprised to find others in the basement. Upstairs everybody talked to each other and joined in with daily projects that were fun and meaningful. Nobody talked to each other in the basement. They were too ashamed, and most felt that the basement was where they really belonged anyway. Those old tapes questioned the love of this new Father, and he began to question whether he was ever adopted in the first place.

He made a few halfhearted attempts to return to the light, but eventually he found a dark corner to lie down in. Then one day a shaft of light penetrated his mind and reason returned. He began to think, "Why not throw myself on the mercy of this person who calls Himself my Father? What do I have to lose? Even if He makes me eat the crumbs that fall from the table, it would be better than this." So he decided to take the risk of climbing those stairs and to face his Father with the truth of what he had done. "Lord," he said, "I knocked over some glasses and broke a pitcher." Without saying a word, his Father took him by the hand and led him into the dining room. To his utter amazement, his Father had prepared for him a banquet. "Welcome home Son," his Father said. "There is therefore now no condemnation for those who are in Christ Jesus" (Romans 8:1 ESV).

Oh the deep, deep love of Jesus, and the matchless grace of God! The door is always open for those who are willing to throw themselves upon the mercy of God. "In love he predestined us for adoption to sonship through Jesus Christ, in accordance with his pleasure and will—to the praise of his glorious grace, which he has freely given us in the One he loves" (Ephesians 1:4–6). He doesn't want us to live self-condemned lives in the basement of shame, guilt, fear, pride, and legalism. He wants us to know that we are adopted, forgiven, and forever alive in Christ, and that we can live every day as beloved children.

I urge you to take seriously this course that will help you live a liberated life under the grace of God and go on to bear much fruit, fruit that will last forever—and equip others to do the same.

Welcome!

Welcome to *The Grace Course*!

The original *Grace Course* has had such an impact on our own lives and ministries and has gone right around the world.

We feel humbled, privileged, and very excited to share this totally revised version with you and are delighted that it is at the center of *The Grace And Freedom Project*, a collaboration between a number of Christian ministries and publishers.

Our intention is to put a tool into your hands that will enable you to see Christians in your church become more fruitful than they could imagine as they allow God's grace to permeate their lives.

This Leader's Guide is designed to give you everything you need to run a highly effective course. We suggest that you get started as follows:

• Register with us for free access to all the additional online info and downloads (below).

• Read these few introductory pages—they will help you understand the scope and intention of the course and how to run it well.

• Watch the teaching sessions on video (available separately) or read the session notes in this Leader's Guide thoroughly.

• Ensure you have grappled with the concepts in your own life and have been through the ministry component (*The Steps To Experiencing God's Grace*) personally before leading others.

Remember that we at Freedom In Christ Ministries are always ready to respond to questions from church leaders so feel free to get in touch.

May God bless you as you lead others into this amazing grace of His!

Steve Goss and the Freedom In Christ team

PLEASE REGISTER AS A USER!

It costs nothing and you will receive

• access to a web area with helpful info for course leaders

• downloads that will make running your course even easier

• publicity material for your *Grace Course*

• *Grace Course* timings calculator

• sample documents for the ministry component of the course.

Register at: www.FreedomInChrist.org/GraceCourse

We never share your contact information with third parties. We will not bombard you with unwanted emails.

> ABOUT THE GRACE COURSE

WHAT IS THE GRACE COURSE?

Jesus said that people would recognize His disciples by their love (John 13:35). Paul said: "For Christ's love compels us" (2 Corinthians 5:14). *The Grace Course* is a tool for churches to help Christians recover their first love for God (see Revelation 2:4) so that they go on to love others and make a great impact on the world. In order for Christians to be motivated purely by love, we have to help them get rid of "false motivators" such as:

SHAME

How we see ourselves determines how we will live. We give mental assent to the truth that we have become "new creations" in Christ (2 Corinthians 5:17), but in practice shame leads us to allow our identity to be determined by our past rather than by what Christ did for us on the cross. Many of us feel that we are "a let-down" to God and other people, that we are fundamentally flawed. This is compounded when we find ourselves stuck in sins that we can't seem to escape from.

GUILT

We know, in theory at least, that salvation is by grace through faith, and that we cannot earn it. But many of us unconsciously fall into the trap of believing in effect that we maintain God's acceptance by working hard and "doing the right things." Guilt conditions us to believe that our ongoing acceptance by God is a product of how well we are performing and makes us behave as if our growth in Christ is primarily up to us. We end up stressed out, burned out or fed up.

FEAR

Some know full well that they are in the grip of fears but have lost hope that they can resolve them. Others don't see themselves as fearful because they have learned to live with their fears, thinking, "That's just how I am." In both cases, fear holds us back from stepping into all that God has for us and from telling others the wonderful news about Jesus and His salvation.

PRIDE

Pride leads us to take charge of our lives and try to control events and other people instead of trusting the God of all wisdom. It leads to anxious performance and burn-out. Pride also turns a living relationship with Jesus into nothing more than dry religion where we put rules above relationship and laws above love and become more concerned about being right than being real. Humility is the gateway to true unity amongst God's people, which is what will lead to the world knowing that the Father sent Jesus (see John 17:21).

A true understanding of God's grace provides the antidote to these false motivators. *The Grace Course* is designed to help Christians understand the mind-blowing benefits of what it means to be God's child: that, no matter what's in the past, we are perfectly acceptable to God; that we don't have to try hard to "act like we think Christians should act;" that we can simply live out of the truth of who we now are—free, unashamed, innocent, victorious, courageous, and calm—so that we humble ourselves before God and bear fruit and humble ourselves before other Christians, working in unity to make disciples and see the nations transformed!

The Grace Course puts the emphasis on *knowing* the truth, not just in our heads but in our hearts. It is full of practical exercises for people to engage with and has a gentle, effective ministry component called *The Steps To Experiencing God's Grace*, and a powerful tool for renewing your mind called *Stronghold-Busting*.

If you can encourage Christians to "do business with God" during *The Grace Course*, you are likely to see them so impacted by a new sense of God's grace that they will go on to live for Him, not because they feel they have to but just because they love Him. And they'll go on to bear lots of fruit, fruit that will last (see John 15:16). Imagine how different your church could be! Imagine what an impact that would make on your community!

WHAT IS THE STRUCTURE OF THE COURSE?

There are eight main teaching sessions followed by a practical ministry component, *The Steps To Experiencing God's Grace*, and a further practical session on how to replace faulty beliefs with the truth from God's Word.

SESSION 1: FREE!
Luke 15:11–31

God's grace means that you are not just forgiven, not just saved. You are completely restored. Deep down inside, you are a totally new person. And God doesn't just love you. He absolutely delights in you, even when you go wrong.

God's love, acceptance, and favor have nothing to do with our behavior, good or bad. But they have everything to do with His grace.

Most Christians don't know what they already have or just who they already are. They know they are saved by grace but slip into thinking that being a disciple of Jesus means somehow having to maintain that favor by doing the right things.

In Christ we are perfectly loved and accepted for who we are, not for what we do. From that position of security, we can make a free choice to serve God because we love Him, and get rid of any other false motivation.

Yet what we do does matter. Sin has horrendous consequences. God has prepared things for each one of us to do and at the end of time He will test what we have done. Anything where our motivation was not love will not count for eternity.

SESSION 2: UNASHAMED!
2 Corinthians 5:21, Hebrews 10:19–22

God is love. Everything God has ever done or ever will do is motivated purely by love. And discipleship is about becoming more and more like Him. So our starting point in any situation is always love—and our middle point and our end point, too!

Out of love, God created human beings and gave us a task to work with Him to continue bringing order out of chaos as we looked after the Earth. He did not make us robots who had to do what He told us to, but instead gave us the ability to make genuine choices which had genuine consequences for good or for ill.

God warned Adam of the consequences of eating from a certain tree: "You will surely die." But, deceived by Satan, Adam chose to disobey, and he and Eve suffered spiritual death—they lost their spiritual connection to God and all that came with it: their significance, their intimate relationship with God, their security. They were cut off from the fellowship with God they had enjoyed. They didn't know Him any more.

There were consequences for all of their descendants too. All of us were born as "sinners" without the spiritual life and connection to God we were designed to have. We instinctively felt shame because we were not the people we were meant to be.

Our sense of shame can be intensified by our upbringing or negative experiences.

Jesus *became* sin and we *became* holy ones. Knowing our new identity resolves shame so that we can be motivated only by love.

SESSION 3: INNOCENT!
Philippians 3:4–6, Colossians 2:13–14, Luke 7:48–50

Most Christians have come to see God as someone whose primary concern is how we behave and we therefore feel constantly guilty because we feel we don't measure up to His expectations.

We think that Jesus came primarily to forgive our sins rather than to give us back the life that Adam lost. We lose sight of the other emphases in the Bible which tell us that Jesus came to set us free from slavery to death, to the flesh, to sin and to Satan.

God does not want us to be motivated by guilt but wants us to know that all of our sins—past, present and future—have been completely and utterly dealt with by Christ's death on the cross so that we can stand confidently before God.

If we do go wrong, God does not want us to feel guilty but does want us to experience godly sorrow that motivates us to walk in the light with Him—totally open and transparent.

It's grace, not guilt, that is the most powerful motivator not to keep sinning.

SESSION 4: VICTORIOUS!

Romans 6:3–14, 7:14–24

What we *do* comes from who we *are*.

When we chose to follow Jesus, we became totally different people to who we were before. We are no longer *sinners*. We are *holy ones*. But truth doesn't set you free unless you *know* it.

We have understood that Jesus' death and resurrection dealt not only with the <u>penalty</u> of sin but also the <u>power</u> of sin. It is now genuinely possible at any given moment to make a choice how to behave and there is a way out of every temptation we face. But if we choose to offer our bodies to sin, we allow evil to reign in our bodies. We can resolve this by submitting to God and resisting the devil. You don't grow into freedom. You take hold of it.

All God has ever wanted of His people is that they obey Him, not because they *have* to but because they *choose* to. Freedom is being put in the position where you can do that.

SESSION 5: COURAGEOUS!

Joshua 1:5–6, Hebrews 13:5–8, 2 Timothy 1:7

God has prepared things for you to do that will make your life count for eternity. He's always looking for ways to help you grow so that you can do them in His strength.

We will experience fear at many points in our lives and it will try to make us hold back from doing what God wants us to do. Courage is not the absence of fear. It's making the right choice in the face of fear. But if we allow fear to dictate our actions, it will imprison us.

We do not have to allow unhealthy fears to control us or set the agenda in our lives because God is all-powerful and everywhere-present and has given us the grace gifts of power, love and sound judgment.

SESSION 6: CALM!

1 Peter 5:6–8, Isaiah 30:15, Psalm 46:10

The uncertainties we face can make us anxious but living in anxiety makes us "double-minded" and unstable and provides an opportunity for Satan to take advantage of us.

If you are feeling habitually anxious, it is a strong indication that you are still trying to handle your life yourself and this is essentially pride.

God's goal for your life is that you become more and more like Him in character. It's not so much about what you *do* but what you're *like*. Humbling yourself under God's mighty hand means cooperating with Him and adjusting your goals to His.

Even though we live in an age of anxiety, we can live without unhealthy anxiety. It comes down to knowing just who our Father God is, trusting His character and ways, and choosing to cooperate with Him.

When we genuinely know God as He is and understand His true character of love, we can cast our anxiety onto Him, leave it with Him, and live free of it.

SESSION 7: FRUITFUL!

Philippians 2:2–8, John 15:1–5, Hebrews 12:5–11, Matthew 11:28–30, Psalm 131

If we want to be fruitful, our focus needs not to be on bearing fruit but on staying connected to Jesus. Apart from Him we can do nothing of any eternal value.

Fruitfulness comes when we submit to God and what He says in His Word, when we set aside our pride and choose to humble ourselves before Him.

God genuinely offers us rest for our souls, a light burden and an easy yoke. We no longer need to try to control events or people but can choose to humble ourselves before God and other people and trust Father God to take care of the things that are outside our control.

The gateway to fruitfulness is brokenness. In His love God uses the difficult situations we encounter to cut away self-centeredness, self-reliance and pride.

The appropriate response to God's grace towards us is to offer our whole selves to Him as a living sacrifice.

SESSION 8: PEACEMAKER!
Matthew 28:18–20, John 13:35, 17:21, 1 Corinthians 5:9–11, Revelation 19:6–8

When you came to Christ, you became part of the most significant body of people that have ever lived. The Church is the body of Christ—we literally are the flesh and blood through whom God works in the world. There is no Plan B.

Our calling is not to condemn people for their issues but to show them the way out. Discipleship is not about telling people what is *wrong* with them. It starts with helping people understand what is *right* with them, now that they are in Christ.

The one thing Jesus prayed for us, who come after His original disciples, is that we would be one "so that the world may know that you have sent me." Maintaining the unity of the Spirit through the bond of peace is a prerequisite for the Church to make the greatest possible impact in this world.

Historically Christians have assumed that unity comes from a common understanding of doctrine. And paradoxically the result has been disunity. Peacemakers unite around their love for Jesus, submit to one another, and are passionate about being part of the Bride of Christ.

And there is cause for great optimism because Revelation 19:7 tells us that the Bride will have made herself ready for the wedding of the Lamb!

THE STEPS TO EXPERIENCING GOD'S GRACE
The Steps To Experiencing God's Grace is a practical session that will help you ensure that the Biblical principles we've looked at in *The Grace Course* become real in your experience.

You will ask the Holy Spirit to help you see areas of sin that are giving the enemy some influence in your life. As you submit to God by acknowledging the issues and turning away from them, you will close the "doors" you opened. At the end of the process you will resist the devil and he will have no option but to flee from you.

All of this is done in a kind and gentle way, and it's just between you and God.

During the process you will be able to identify areas where your beliefs have been out of line with what is actually true according to God's Word, the Bible. The *Stronghold-Busting* Session will equip you with a simple method to demolish those strongholds, one that you can use for the rest of your life whenever you become aware that your belief system is off-kilter with the Bible.

STRONGHOLD-BUSTING SESSION
Romans 12:1–2, 2 Corinthians 10:3–5, Ephesians 2:1–3, Colossians 2:8

We are transformed by the renewing of our mind, a lifelong process of recognizing faulty thinking we have developed by comparing it to the truth in God's Word, and then consciously choosing to bring our thinking into line with what God says is true.

Faulty beliefs that have become deeply ingrained are referred to as "strongholds" by Paul. They matter because our actions always flow from our beliefs and strongholds lead us to make bad choices and ultimately prevent us from experiencing the abundant life that God intends.

"Stronghold-Busting" is a simple methodology that will enable you to demolish the strongholds in your thinking. It is straightforward but does require sustained effort over a period of six weeks or so. For many participants on *The Grace Course*, it is the element that brings the most lasting change and helps them go on to become genuinely fruitful disciples of Jesus.

> WHAT HAS CHANGED IN THIS REVISED VERSION?

The original *Grace Course* was incredibly well received and translated into many languages. We are so grateful to leaders from around the world who fed back to us various comments on the content and made suggestions. In making this revised version, we have endeavored to take the comments and feedback into account while preserving the essential elements of the original course. Every part of the course has been revised, but the main changes are described below.

Despite all the rehearsals and practice, when we recorded the six sessions in the original *Grace Course*, we were enjoying ourselves so much, we ended up making them significantly longer than we had intended. The result was that small groups found it very difficult to go through a session in an evening, and most split each session over two weeks, which made it somewhat unwieldy. Rather than simply reduce the content, we decided to take the course apart and rebuild it from first principles—and we applied an iron discipline to our recording sessions to ensure that we kept to time!

The essential teaching principles remain the same with the parable of the prodigal son at the heart. We have, however, comprehensively revised the teaching, changed its order somewhat, and expanded it, especially in the areas of anxiety and the importance of taking our place alongside our brothers and sisters in the Church. In one area—teaching on the Old Testament Law—we have reduced the teaching (but have included it in full in *The Grace Connection*, the accompanying book).

In order to ensure that each session is not too long, we have increased the number of main teaching sessions from six to eight. Additionally, we have created a separate "Stronghold-Busting" session that is designed to accompany the ministry component, *The Steps To Experiencing God's Grace*, which has also been completely revised and adapted to reflect the teaching emphases of the main course. It is the content of this session that is often the key to ongoing transformation and fruitfulness, and we hope that this separate session will be a constant guide to disciples until renewing their mind to God's Word becomes second nature.

The Pause For Thought questions have been thoroughly revised, and a new Reflect section is included at the end of each session to make space for personal response to what has been taught.

We are excited to have been able to add some hugely significant elements to the total "package," in order to increase the ways that people can connect with the teaching. It has been a privilege to work with RightNowMedia to produce *The Wonder Of Grace*, a brand new video series that can serve as an excellent introduction to *The Grace Course*, and to produce for YouVersion a brand new daily devotional—*Daily Nuggets Of Grace*—to accompany participants on their *Grace Course* journey.

We have also been able to have two books published that take participants deeper in the principles we teach. Rich Miller has written a revised edition of his excellent devotional, *40 Days Of Grace*. Now titled *The Wonder Of Grace: A 40-Day Devotional Journey*, it is designed to help participants focus on the principles in the six weeks or so after they finish the course, and Steve Goss has written a new book, *The Grace Connection*, that expands on the teaching in the course and presents it in a slightly different way.

> HOW DOES THE GRACE COURSE WORK TOGETHER WITH THE FREEDOM IN CHRIST COURSE?

The Freedom In Christ Course is a bestselling course consisting of ten sessions plus *The Steps To Freedom In Christ* ministry component—there are further details on page 193 or visit www.FreedomInChrist.org. The look and feel of *The Grace Course* is modeled on *The Freedom In Christ Course*, so it will be instantly familiar to previous users.

The Grace Course can stand alone but is also designed to work well with *The Freedom In Christ Course*. They very much complement each other.

The overall theme running through both courses could be characterized as, "know the truth and the truth will set you free." Both courses have similar main emphases: knowing who you are in Christ and the importance of renewing the mind.

With ten sessions, *The Freedom In Christ* Course is more comprehensive. In particular, it has more to say on the crucial areas of why we need to forgive others, the battle for our minds, recognizing that all of us are predisposed to a particular worldview, and understanding how to bring our goals into line with God's goals for our lives. It tends to draw from the epistles a little more than the Gospels. *The Grace Course*, on the other hand, covers some key areas in a lot more depth than *The Freedom In Christ Course*: shame; guilt; fear; anxiety; pride; and ministering out of rest. It tends to draw from the Gospels a little more than the epistles.

Churches report that the two courses work together extremely well. Leaders tell us that, having experienced one course, people usually want to go on and do the other, and it would be highly beneficial for them to do so.

Nearly all tell us that they use both courses, for example by running one course for a period followed in the next period by the other course, giving participants the opportunity to do both.

So, if you choose to use both courses, our recommendation is that you do not worry too much which order you do them in. We would, however, recommend that, if you do *The Grace Course* first, you consider giving participants an opportunity to go through *The Steps To Freedom In Christ* (the ministry component from *The Freedom In Christ Course*) before they go through *The Steps To Experiencing God's Grace* (the ministry component from *The Grace Course*). It would also be beneficial if possible to show the video of Session 7—"Forgiving From The Heart"—from *The Freedom In Christ Course* during the Away Day retreat for *The Grace Course* because forgiveness is an integral part of the ministry components for both courses and is covered much more comprehensively in *The Freedom In Christ Course*. There is more information on this on page 193.

In summary

- Each of the courses stands alone so can run perfectly well without the other.

- There are real benefits to participants if they do both courses.

- If participants do *The Grace Course* on its own or before *The Freedom In Christ Course*, consider finding a way for them to do *The Steps To Freedom In Christ* and Session 7—"Forgiving From The Heart"—from *The Freedom In Christ Course*.

> HOW CAN THE GRACE COURSE BE USED?

The Grace Course works equally well with those who have just become Christians and those who have been Christians a long time. It has been designed to be flexible enough to use in a variety of church situations:

IN SMALL GROUPS

This is how most churches use our discipleship resources. If people miss a session, make sure that they have access to the videos so that they can catch up.

We recommend that, where possible, small groups use the teaching sessions on video and that you use the Pause For Thought discussion questions. Each small group session is designed to last two hours and you will find a detailed time plan for each session in this Leader's Guide.

It works equally well in face-to-face or online small groups.

SYSTEMATIC PREACHING WITH SMALL GROUP FOLLOW-UP

Each of the Word sections can be delivered as a straight talk (in person or via video). You could, therefore, use them as a main church teaching program (for example in a Sunday service or US Sunday school program). This could be followed up in small groups during the week if there is no opportunity for group discussion.

MID-WEEK MEETING

In a mid-week setting where there are no established small groups, you could bring everyone together and deliver the talk (in person or via the videos) and then divide people into groups for the group discussion questions. Alternatively, you could deliver the talk in sections, allowing the groups to discuss the Pause For Thought questions as you go.

ALONGSIDE AN OUTREACH COURSE

It is possible to combine the course with an outreach course such as Alpha. You could bring both groups together for a meal before sending the not-yet Christians into the outreach course and new Christians into *The Grace Course*. Even if people have not become Christians on the outreach course, this should not preclude them from going on to *The Grace Course*, which will show them clearly in the first couple of sessions the differences that take place when someone becomes a Christian.

ONE-ON-ONE DISCIPLING

It is time-consuming to run the course for just one person but it works very well indeed. It's a great way to disciple a new convert or a mentoring tool for those who have been Christians for a while.

> WHICH METHOD DO YOU RECOMMEND?

Freedom In Christ Ministries has been producing resources for churches around the world since 1988, all designed to help Christians become fruitful disciples. We have found that by far the most effective way for most people to learn in a church environment is in a small group where they are encouraged to discuss what is being taught. In preparing *The Grace Course* our focus has primarily been on creating a small group resource but you will find it will work well in any of the ways outlined above.

> RUNNING YOUR COURSE WHAT MATERIALS ARE REQUIRED?

The Grace Course has three core elements and four additional optional elements. They are listed below and further information (including how to order) can be found at freedominchrist.org/GraceCourse and at GraceAndFreedomProject.com

Your national Freedom In Christ office can supply most elements and will be very pleased to help you with any questions you may have. For contact details please go to freedominchrist.org.

> CORE ELEMENTS

LEADER'S GUIDE

We recommend that everyone leading a small group has their own copy of this Leader's Guide. It contains a guide to running each session, the teaching content of each session, discussion questions, etc.

It is published by Bethany House in North America and by Freedom In Christ Ministries International in the rest of the world. Versions are available in different languages.

PARTICIPANT'S GUIDE

Each participant will need a copy of the Participant's Guide which contains notes for each session, Pause For Thought questions, and the ministry component, *The Steps To Experiencing God's Grace*.

It is published by Bethany House in North America and by Freedom In Christ Ministries International in the rest of the world. Versions are available in different languages.

VIDEO PRESENTATIONS

Most churches use the video presentations to teach *The Grace Course* and they are also helpful to watch even if you are planning to present the course yourself using the notes from the Leader's Guide. We envisage that the main teaching videos will be watched by a small group all together but participants can also engage with it—perhaps to go through it again—on their own.

The videos are presented by Nancy Maldonado, Leisha Lyn-Cook, Rob Davies, and Josh Shaarda and the Participant's Guide has a section that introduces them

They also feature testimonies from people from around the world that illustrate the teaching points being made. There are a variety of English accents and you will almost certainly find that participants will struggle to understand one or two of them that are particularly different from your local English accent. The streamed versions of the videos contain closed captions / subtitles in English and you may like to consider turning these on to aid comprehension.

The streamed versions of the videos also contain captions in other languages—these are being added to constantly as new translations become available.

Available to stream from Freedom In Christ's Discipleship Hub, and from RightNowMedia, and available in North America on DVD (published by Bethany House).

For information on the different elements and where to get them, please go to www.GraceandFreedom Project.com (more info on the following page).

> THE GRACE AND FREEDOM PROJECT

The Grace Course is at the heart of *The Grace and Freedom Project*, a collaboration between a number of leading producers of discipleship and devotional resources.

That means there are some wonderful optional additional resources for participants to take advantage of as they go through *The Grace Course.*

THE WONDER OF GRACE VIDEO SERIES

An 8-session series of short, punchy videos presented by Sidhara Udalagama that cover key themes from *The Grace Course* and are designed to challenge and surprise participants as they grasp that grace is totally counter-intuitive but essential to understand if they really want to make their life count for Jesus. The themes of the sessions correspond to the main *Grace Course* sessions and participants are recommended to watch them in advance of the corresponding *Grace Course* session as a compelling introduction.

Available to stream from Freedom In Christ's Discipleship Hub (free of charge for those who have purchased *The Grace Course* videos on the platform), and from RightNowMedia.

DAILY NUGGETS OF GRACE YOUVERSION DEVOTIONAL

A 56-day (8-week) daily devotional designed to accompany participants on their journey through *The Grace Course*. It consists of short thought-provoking messages to begin each day. Participants are encouraged to begin it on the day they attend the first session of *The Grace Course*. They will then be able to go through seven daily devotionals on the theme of that session. The devotionals are instrumental in reinforcing what has been taught and encouraging participants to engage with it.

Available on The Bible App from YouVersion—search for "Daily Nuggets Of Grace." There is currently no charge for this.

THE GRACE CONNECTION BY STEVE GOSS

A book that sums up the principles of grace and freedom outlined in the other resources. Written by Steve Goss, it will help you connect with grace at a deeper level than ever before and know what it means to take hold of your freedom in Christ.

Published by Freedom In Christ Ministries International. Kindle version available.

THE WONDER OF GRACE: A 40-DAY DEVOTIONAL JOURNEY BY RICH MILLER

A revised and updated version of *40 Days Of Grace*, the devotional book by Rich Miller that has been so popular with participants on the original *Grace Course*. It is designed to be used directly after *The Grace Course* for a six-week period and will help participants process the principles they learned and put them into practice.

Published by Freedom In Christ Ministries International. Gift edition published by Christian Art Gifts.

Scan the QR code to find out more or go to www.Grace andFreedomProject.com.

> HOW DO I LEAD A TEACHING SESSION?

We recommend that you start with coffee and get people to chat and mingle for a while.

Each main teaching session follows the same format and contains the following elements:

LEADER'S NOTES

An introduction for the leader of the session to help you prepare.

CONNECT

This opening time is about connecting with God and with each other. It typically consists of an open question designed to help people get to know each other, and a question that directs people's thoughts toward God.

During this part of the session, it's much more important to encourage group participation and interaction than to do any teaching.

You might like to include sung worship here too, or play a worship song.

If your participants are using *The Wonder Of Grace* videos to prepare for each session, you might simply ask them for their comments on what they have seen.

Or you might invite feedback from the previous session. What struck people particularly from last week? Have they benefited from what they learned during the week in any practical ways? Have they been using the *Daily Nuggets Of Grace* devotional or reading *The Grace Connection* book?

But you almost certainly won't have time to do all of those things!

PRAYER AND DECLARATION

This is an opportunity to encourage people to pray together out loud and then to make a declaration. A prayer is said to God while a declaration is spoken out to the spiritual world in general.

A recurring theme in the course is that, as new creations in Christ, participants have the ability and responsibility to take charge of their Christian life, which includes taking a stand against their spiritual enemies. The declaration at the start of each session is to help participants get used to wielding the power and authority they have in Christ. It may well be a new concept for many, but encourage everyone to declare it boldly as the children of God they are!

FOCUS TRUTH AND VERSE

Introduce the Focus Verse and the Focus Truth for the session. There is no need to say more than is written in the Leader's Guide. Then go straight into the Word section.

WORD

This is the main part of each session. Each talk lasts between 33 and 35 minutes in total (excluding Pause For Thought discussions) but is split into three parts of between 9 and 14 minutes separated by Pause For Thought discussions. This includes filmed testimonies on the videos that help to illustrate the main points.

We envisage that the teaching will be delivered as part of your session and that is the method we assume in this Leader's Guide. However, some choose to ask participants to watch the video in advance of the session and then devote the face-to-face time to fellowship and discussing the Pause For Thought questions. You may like to consider that as an option.

If you choose to present the material yourself, you will find the talk written out in full in this Leader's Guide together with some useful additional material. We recommend that you stick as closely as possible to the notes (but without reciting them parrot fashion), ideally supplementing them with illustrations from your own experience to replace those of the video presenters.

Play the video or start the talk, pausing for discussion at the Pause For Thought questions as indicated. If you are presenting yourself, keep an eye on time and try to resist the temptation to deviate too much from the notes so that the main points are not lost. The small group time plans for each session will help with timekeeping. Registered users can download a customizable version of these on a spreadsheet so that you can insert your own start time and adjust the timings to your own preferences.

PAUSE FOR THOUGHT DISCUSSIONS

The Word section contains two groups of Pause For Thought questions between sections and one Reflect time at the end (see below). It is in these times that the real learning often takes place, and they are of crucial importance.

In the time plan at the beginning of each session, we have suggested timings—do guard against shortening them if at all possible. For settings where the Word section has been delivered elsewhere (for example, in a Sunday service) and follow-up only is required, you can plan a session based exclusively on the Pause For Thought and Reflect times. It is not necessary for people to go through all of the questions listed. The most important thing is that they spend the time grappling with what has been taught, and if that means looking at just one question in more depth, that's fine.

If your group is larger than eight, split people down into subgroups of no more than seven or eight for the discussions and mix the groups up each week. Occasionally it is helpful to split people up by gender. For variety, consider some discussions in smaller groups of three to four to allow quieter ones to talk. As a leader of a discussion group, one of your main roles is to try to get others to talk. Don't be afraid of silences and feel you have to fill them.

In addition to the questions given, you could start any Pause For Thought with the following open questions:

- What do you think about what you just heard?
- Was there anything you heard that you didn't understand or that needs further clarification?
- How do you think what you have heard applies to you?

You do not have to cover every Pause For Thought question. It can be more valuable to go into depth on one question than cover three questions in a cursory manner. Try not to let the conversation wander too far from the main points and keep an eye on the time (a suggested time for each Pause For Thought section is given at the start of each session). Draw the discussion to a close at the appropriate time by summarizing briefly.

REFLECT

Whereas Pause For Thoughts are discussions designed for groups, the aim of a Reflect time is to give individuals an opportunity to respond to what the Holy Spirit is saying to them personally. Ideally they will feel like unhurried times in God's presence during which key truths sink in and people make their own response to Him. Sometimes there is an element of interaction with others. At other times it's more about spending time quietly with God. This can feel a little strange to some but it is good to encourage them in this. It can help to play soft instrumental worship music during these times (music with words or music that is too lively can be distracting however).

> WHAT IS THE MINISTRY COMPONENT?

The Steps To Freedom In Christ is a structured process of prayer and repentance written by Dr. Neil T. Anderson (founder of Freedom In Christ Ministries) which has been used by millions of people around the world. It has been published in many languages and formats and is the ministry component of *The Freedom In Christ Course*.

The ministry component of *The Grace Course* is a similar process called *The Steps To Experiencing God's Grace*. It is based on the same principles of the believer taking responsibility for their life and choosing to submit to God and resist the devil (James 4:7).

Both processes work in a similar way. The person going through (whom we will call "the freedom seeker") takes responsibility for their life and growth by asking the Holy Spirit to show them any area in their life where an issue needs to be resolved. They then choose to repent of everything He shows them, thus removing any grounds the enemy may have had in their life. It is a very straight-forward approach that is kind and gentle—but amazingly effective. Both have seven steps, each of which deals with a specific area of the freedom seeker's life. Each step starts with a biblically-based prayer of repentance which the freedom seeker prays as a general preliminary, asking the Holy Spirit to bring to mind the specific areas that apply to them. Then there are particular instances listed and a short written prayer of renunciation which the freedom seeker will use to deal with specific areas they want to renounce. Some sections also include doctrinal affirmations which are declarations of the freedom seeker's choice and acceptance of primary Scriptural truth set out in a very straightforward way.

We recommend where possible that participants on *The Grace Course* go through *The Steps To Freedom In Christ* before *The Steps To Experiencing God's Grace*. Many will already have been through them as part of *The Freedom In Christ Course*, but if you have a group that has not done that course, you could choose to do *The Steps To Freedom In Christ* instead of *The Steps To Experiencing God's Grace* after Session 8 and then come back to *The Steps To Experiencing God's Grace* at a later date. In order to do that, you would need to purchase *The Steps To Freedom In Christ* book for participants and use *The Steps To Freedom In Christ* video which guides a group through the process. We recognize that this involves a small amount of additional cost but if you want to make these principles a "way of life" in your church, it would be well worth it. It is not, however, essential to do this and you can run *The Grace Course* just as it is and expect great results!

It is possible for people to go through the process either in the context of a group Away Day retreat or in an individual "freedom appointment" in the context of their local church. There is more information in *The Steps To Experiencing God's Grace* section.

> RENEWING THE MIND—"STRONGHOLD-BUSTING"

In Romans 12:2 (ESV), Paul tells us what it is that will cause transformation in a Christian: "be transformed by the renewal of your mind." "Transformed" is a strong word. Its literal meaning is "metamorphosis," the change a caterpillar undergoes in order to become a butterfly.

Most people will come to *The Grace Course* expecting to "receive," and of course, we expect them to receive some really helpful teaching. But it's unlikely that they will be transformed if all they do is "receive." In order to be transformed, they have to work on the renewal of their mind, which means throwing out old ways of thinking based on lies they have come to believe and replacing those ways of thinking with what God tells us is really true in His Word.

All of us have been conditioned by past experiences to believe things that do not line up completely with God's Word. Given that God's Word is the truth, we can legitimately call these false beliefs "lies." When a lie becomes deeply ingrained it becomes a "stronghold," a habitual way of thinking that is inconsistent with what God says in His Word (or, if you prefer, any wrong belief or action that has a "strong hold" on you). It's like having a solid wall in your mind that prevents you from going the way God wants you to.

Directly after *The Steps To Experiencing God's Grace* session, we introduce a strategy called "Stronghold-Busting." It is a forty-day process of replacing lies with truth. Why forty days? Psychologists tell us that it takes around six weeks to form or break a habit. Once you have dealt with any footholds of the enemy, a mental stronghold is simply a habitual way of thinking.

We cannot emphasize enough how significant Stronghold-Busting is to participants who actively engage with it. They really are transformed at a deep, core level. The challenge is to help people believe that genuine transformation really will take place so that they will follow through on the process.

Please plan how you are going to run the Stronghold-Busting session, and, whatever you do, do not be tempted to miss it. It is an absolutely fundamental and essential part of the course. The reason we have put it into a separate session is to give you flexibility. Some people will want to run it on their Away Day directly after the steps. Others may want to run a ninth teaching session in the week following the Away Day.

> HINTS & TIPS

Church and course leaders—send a message that "this is for everyone" by going through the teaching and the ministry component and writing a Stronghold-Buster yourself first.

Surround your course with prayer. It is a vital part of preparation for your course and should not stop once the course gets underway. If you can assemble a group of people to pray for your course, you will really notice the difference. Consider meeting before each session for prayer with another leader.

Emphasize that every participant will need to apply ongoing effort to maintain the freedom gained and continue to grow as a disciple.

Take it slowly—our courses are not generally something that a church does just once but tend to become a regular part of church life. As such, it is worth taking the time and effort at the outset to make sure that the courses run as well as they possibly can.

Look out for the enemy's attack—often through the least expected people.

Decide early on how you are going to approach running *The Steps To Experiencing God's Grace* (there are more details in *The Steps To Experiencing God's Grace* session). If you decide on the Away Day retreat approach, ensure that you book a suitable venue in good time and give everyone the date as early as you can. Make sure participants understand that this is an integral part of the course and not to be missed!

Keep emphasizing that this is discipleship for everyone—not just for "hard cases" or any particular section of the church.

"Transformed lives transform lives"—be prepared for the course to make a positive difference throughout your church and beyond as people come to a fresh understanding of God's grace. Think about how it could impact your community as Christians discover afresh for themselves that Jesus really is the answer to the issues out there.

Remember that Freedom In Christ Ministries exists to equip leaders. Don't hesitate to get in touch if you have a question or need any advice.

PERSONAL PRAYER OF PREPARATION

God, You're the bedrock under my feet and I depend completely on You. You protect me and clear the ground under me so that my footing is firm. You're the one true and living God. You're a tower of salvation, a shield to all who trust in You, my refuge and my deliverer.

I humbly accept Your call to lead this *Grace Course*. On my own I can do nothing whatsoever that will make a difference but I stand in the truth that all authority in heaven and earth has been given to the resurrected Christ, and because I am in Christ, I share that authority in order to make disciples and set prisoners free.

Thank You that You have cleansed me and washed away my sin. As I declare Your Word in Your strength and power, please fill me afresh with Your Holy Spirit.

Strengthen me by Your Spirit, so that I'll be able to take in to a greater degree the extravagant dimensions of Your love and grace and pass that on to others on the course. I declare that I have a spirit of power and love and a sound mind, and that the Word of Christ dwells in me richly. I've been made holy by Your Word of Truth. The anointing I've received from You abides in me.

Your Word is an indispensable weapon to me, and in the same way, prayer is essential in ongoing warfare. So I declare that because I've made You my dwelling place, no evil shall come upon me. Your promise is that You will give Your angels charge over all that concerns me, and You will keep me in all my ways.

I welcome the kingdom of the Lord Jesus Christ afresh today into my life, my home, my family, my work, and into all I do within the ministry of making disciples in my church.

I pray all of this in the name of Jesus Christ. Amen.

Based on: 1 John 4:4; 2 Samuel 22; Psalm 51; Psalm 19:14; Ephesians 3:16; 2 Timothy 1:7; Colossians 3:16; John 17:17; 1 John 2:27; Ephesians 3:8; Psalm 91:9–11; 2 Corinthians 4:1–7.

TEAM DECLARATION

We declare that Jesus is our Lord. He's greater than the one who is in the world and He came to destroy all the devil's works, having triumphed over him by the cross.

We declare that God has given us *The Grace Course* at this time to share His Word, and the gates of hell will not prevail against it. The words that come out of God's mouth will not return empty-handed. They'll do the work He sent them to do.

As those who are seated in the heavenly realms, we agree that Satan and every enemy of the Lord Jesus must not in any way interfere with the running of this course. We commit the place where the sessions will take place to Jesus. We cleanse it in Jesus' name from any impure thing.

We declare that the truth of God's mighty Word will be planted and established in [name your church or organization] and that those who come will know the truth and be set free. We will use our powerful God-given tools for tearing down barriers erected against the truth of God, and for building lives of obedience into maturity.

We announce that what God has promised gets stamped with the "yes" of Jesus. We declare that our God can do anything—far more than we could ever imagine or guess or request. Glory to God in the Church! Glory down all the generations forever and ever!

God is striding ahead of us. He's right there with us. He won't let us down. He won't leave us. We won't be intimidated and we won't worry. The battle belongs to Him!

Based on: Colossians 2:15; John 10:10; John 8:32; Matthew 16:18; Isaiah 55:11; 2 Corinthians 10:4; 2 Corinthians 1:20; Ephesians 3; Deuteronomy 31:8, 1 Samuel 17:47.

> INTRODUCTION TO THE WORD SECTION

We have set out below full scripts for the teaching for each session. This is for your reference but also so that you can teach the sessions yourself if you choose to.

We have based the scripts largely on what the video presenters say. Much of the impact comes from their use of personal stories that illustrate the key points. We have retained many of these, putting them in italics, the idea being that, if possible, you replace them with your own stories.

Occasionally we have replaced a presenter's story with a more generic illustration that we feel will make it easier for you to deliver the teaching yourself.

FREEDOM
IN CHRIST

session **01**

FREE!

OBJECTIVE

To understand that what really matters to God
is not only what we do but why we do it.

LEADER'S NOTES

THE THEME RUNNING THROUGH THIS FIRST SESSION COULD BE DEFINED AS "SONSHIP VERSUS SLAVERY."

We will focus on the story Jesus told that is generally known as the parable of the prodigal son. We prefer to call it the parable of the two sons because the context makes clear that the focus of the story is not so much the younger son who went astray but rather the elder brother who appeared outwardly to be doing everything right yet inwardly was far away from his father.

The story appears in a string of parables in Luke 15 dealing with things that are lost: the parable of the lost sheep, the parable of the lost coin, and then this one, which could easily be entitled the parable of the lost son. The question is, which of the sons was lost— the younger, the elder, or both? By the end of the story, it's clear that the younger son, though once lost, has now been found, but the elder son is still lost.

Although the elder son is free to enjoy right now everything his father owns, he is deceived into thinking he has to "slave away" to earn it as a future reward. This attitude keeps him from intimacy with the father and makes him behave in ways that are more in keeping with a hired hand who "slaves away" rather than the son he is.

The key point we want to help participants understand is that they are not just in the position the younger son was in immediately upon his return, that of a "forgiven sinner," someone who has been forgiven but is still essentially the same no-good person they always were. We want them to know that, even though they don't deserve it, they have become "sons" with all the authority, responsibility and privilege that implies. From their position as sons, they are free to choose whether to live for the father or not. But when you understand just what this father is like and what he has done, why on earth wouldn't you want to serve him?

We finish the session with something of a paradox. Having said that we don't need to "slave away" for God, we note that the New Testament actually often gives a positive slant to the word *slave* (*doulos* in the Greek), with Paul, for example, calling himself a "slave of Christ" (Romans 1:1 NLT). Even though we are free not to serve Him, when we understand how good He is and how loving He is, of our own free will we can commit ourselves to becoming His bondslaves.

> THE DANGER OF ANTINOMIANISM

Antinomianism is an old heresy that has afflicted the Church through the ages. The term means "anti-law" and was coined by Martin Luther to refer to the practice of pushing the doctrine of justification by faith alone too far and saying, in effect, that since Christians are saved by faith alone, it does not matter at all how they behave.

The teaching in this session may sound to some as if it is heading in that direction but that is categorically not the case. Encourage any who express concern to bear with it and reassure them that, as the course develops, they will see the whole picture.

D. Martyn Lloyd-Jones, the great proponent of evangelical theology and minister of Westminster Chapel in London, who was prominent in the middle of the Twentieth Century, said:

> "There is no better test as to whether a man is really preaching the New Testament gospel than this, that some people might misunderstand it and misinterpret it that it really amounts to this: that because you are saved by grace alone, it does not really matter at all WHAT you do, you can go on sinning all you like. . . ."

Note how he says that interpreting gospel preaching as meaning that it doesn't matter how you behave is to misunderstand it. His point is that, if you don't find some people misinterpreting your teaching in this way, then you are not actually preaching the true gospel of grace. He goes on to say even more directly (and in capital letters!):

> "I would say to all preachers: IF YOUR PREACHING OF SALVATION HAS NOT BEEN MISUNDERSTOOD IN THAT WAY, THEN YOU HAD BETTER EXAMINE YOUR SERMONS AGAIN, and you had better make sure that you really ARE preaching the salvation that is proclaimed in the New Testament."[1]

Our objective in this course is to help people receive a revelation of God's grace. Most people find that revelation profoundly shocking when it comes. On the face of it, it may seem that we can behave however we like, but anyone who persists in that way of thinking has not had a genuine revelation of grace. Those who truly understand it go in the opposite direction: they fall more in love with God and want to serve Him with all that they are and have.

---

1 D. Martyn Lloyd-Jones, Romans, An Exposition of Chapter 6, The New Man, (Grand Rapids: Zondervan, 1973), pages 9–10.

SMALL GROUP TIMINGS

The following plan is designed to help those leading the course in small groups. It assumes a meeting of around ninety minutes in length, and suggests how long each part of the session should last, with an indication of cumulative elapsed time. You will find a time plan in each session. The second column shows the time allocated to each individual element in minutes and seconds. The third column shows the total elapsed time in hours and minutes.

Session 1	Minutes:Seconds	Hours:Minutes
Welcome, Focus, Connect	15:00	00:15
Word Part A	13:30	00:28
Pause For Thought 1	14:00	00:42
Word Part B	09:30	00:52
Pause For Thought 2	13:45	01:05
Word Part C	10:15	01:16
Reflect	14:00	01:30

The time allocated for the Word sections is based on the length of the corresponding section of the videos.

Registered users of the course (see page 11) can download an Excel spreadsheet with these timings. Simply enter your own start time, adjust the length of the various components if desired and you will have a timed plan of your session.

FOCUS VERSE

We love because he first loved us.

1 John 4:19

 FOCUS TRUTH

In Christ we are perfectly loved and accepted for who we are, not what we do. From that position of security, we can make a free choice to serve God because we love Him, and get rid of any other false motivation.

 CONNECT

One definition of *grace* is "getting what you don't deserve." Tell about a time you got what you didn't deserve. What did you deserve? What did you actually get?

If you watched *The Wonder Of Grace* introductory video for this session, what was the main thing that struck you?

PRAYER & DECLARATION

Heavenly Father, Thank You that the grace You showed us when Jesus went to the cross is available to us day by day. We pray today that You will guide us into all truth, reveal to us the strongholds in our minds, and help us to renew our minds, so that we will be transformed. We want to be disciples who bear much fruit. We choose to set our hope fully on the grace to be given to us when Jesus Christ is revealed. In His name. Amen.

We declare that, even though we live in the world, we do not wage war as the world does—we fight with weapons which have divine power! For every unhelpful way of thinking that has a "strong hold" on us, we choose to believe God's clear promise that we can demolish them. Not just cope with them, work around them, or do them a bit of damage. Demolish them! And in so doing we will be transformed by the renewing of our minds.

─O WORD

> INTRODUCTION

Welcome to *The Grace Course*!

What's your favorite hymn? Different people like different ones. If you were a dentist you might perhaps go for "Crown Him With Many Crowns." If you were a paramedic, you might be whistling "Revive Us Again." I guess if you were a baker it would be "When The Roll Is Called Up Yonder!"

For many people, their favorite hymn is "Amazing Grace:" "Amazing grace how sweet the sound that saved a wretch like me." Apparently John Newton's 250-year-old hymn is sung around 10 million times a year. I've been a Christian a long time, and I think I have probably sung it nearly as many times myself!

This course is all about grace. Paul tells us in Romans 5:2 that we have obtained by faith "our introduction . . . into this grace in which we stand" (NASB). When I first became a Christian, I understood grace as being primarily about God's love when He sent Jesus to die for me. Peter tells us that God wants us to "grow in the grace and knowledge of our Lord and Savior Jesus Christ" (2 Peter 3:18). The grace that God wants us to experience is for every moment of every day, and that's what this course is about.

And, although John Newton's great hymn starts by talking about the grace that saved us the moment we first turned to Christ, it goes on to say:

Through many dangers, toils and snares I have already come;

'Tis Grace that brought me safe thus far And Grace will lead me home.

The objective of the course is to help you know what it means to experience God's grace every day so that you can be fruitful to the fullest possible extent. And that's an exciting prospect.

[Do you have a story of God's grace and what it has meant in your life that you could share at this point?]

Grace is so needed in the Church. In preparation for writing a book on legalism and grace with Dr. Neil Anderson and Paul Travis, we contracted the George Barna Research Group to do a scientific survey of American Christianity. We asked followers of Christ to respond to six statements. One of them was: "The Christian life is well–summed up as trying hard to obey God's commands." To our astonishment, we discovered that 82 percent of those surveyed agreed with that statement; 57 percent strongly agreed! Well, there's nothing wrong with that statement aside from the fact that it's totally wrong! There's nothing in there about grace . . . about faith . . . about love . . . about relationship. There's nothing in there about Jesus! Our conclusion was—and remains—that law-based living rather than grace-based living is endemic in the Church.

> UNDERSTANDING GRACE

To get us started, I want to ask you to consider a question. Jesus said, "If you love me, you will obey my commands" (John 14:15 NCV). Imagine Him saying that personally just to you. How do you hear Him saying it? What expression is on His face? This? . . . Or this? . . . What expression is in His voice? Before we finish this session, we'll do our best to resolve that question.

> THE STORY OF THE TWO BROTHERS

Let's look now at a story that Jesus told that will really help us come to grips with God's grace.

THE YOUNGER BROTHER

And he said, "There was a man who had two sons. The younger of them said to his father, 'Father, give me my share of the estate.'"

Luke 15:11–12 ESV

Do you realize that he might as well have said, "I wish you were dead"? A father's inheritance was to come to his sons after his death. But this son just couldn't wait.

"So he divided his property between them. Not long after that, the younger son got together all he had, set off for a distant country and there squandered his wealth in wild living. After he had spent everything, there was a severe famine in that whole country, and he began to be in need. So he went and hired himself out to a citizen of that country, who sent him to his fields to feed pigs. He longed to fill his stomach with the pods that the pigs were eating, but no one gave him anything.

"When he came to his senses, he said, 'How many of my father's hired servants have food to spare, and here I am starving to death! I will set out and go back to my father and say to him: Father, I have sinned against heaven and against you. I am no longer worthy to be called your son; make me like one of your hired servants.' So he got up and went to his father."

Luke 15:12–20

The younger boy had turned his back completely on his father and the way of life he had been brought up in.

What Jesus is doing here is painting a picture of someone whose behavior was the worst imaginable in his culture. He showed no respect whatsoever for his father. He engaged in adultery, spending money on prostitutes. Then, when he had no money left, he even stooped so low as to take a job looking after the animal that, to Jews, represented the height of uncleanness—pigs. It's difficult to imagine that he could have behaved any worse, or any less deservingly of his title as son. He himself knew that he had blown it completely and decided to return to his Father, not expecting to be received as a son but hoping simply for a job as a hired hand, one who would have to earn anything that might come from the father.

"But while he was still a long way off, his father saw him and was filled with compassion for him; he ran to his son, threw his arms around him, and kissed him."

Luke 15:20

Note that the father ran—in that culture, wealthy men never did that. Love for his son overcame all the social norms.

"And the son said to him, 'Father, I have sinned against heaven and against you. I am no longer worthy to be called your son.'"

Luke 15:21

Was that true, that his sin made him no longer worthy to be called a son? Yes, undoubtedly, though of course nothing could change the fact that he was a son and always would be. But watch how the father reacts: It's almost as if he was not even listening to the words of his son's well-rehearsed confession. The father knew the son's heart and that he was sorry and had come back. And that's all that mattered!

"But the father said to his servants, 'Quick! Bring the best robe and put it on him. Put a ring on his finger and sandals on his feet. Bring the fattened calf and kill it. [This is the only character in the story for whom the whole thing is really bad news!] Let's have a feast and celebrate. For this son of mine was dead and is alive again; he was lost and is found.' So they began to celebrate."

Luke 15:22–24

The son expected to be disowned or at best to be severely punished—and that would have been what he deserved. Yet the father immediately embraces this smelly, dirty, broken individual, puts the best clothes on him and throws a party to end all parties!

He also gives him three things that had great significance:

First, the robe wasn't any old robe but was the best robe in the house, perhaps the father's own robe. It symbolized that the son had once again been given the right to enjoy the place of "right standing" with the father. He had always been loved, but now he was completely restored.

Second, the ring would have been a signet-type ring that would make a mark on official documents and could be instantly recognizable as the father's mark. Without that mark or seal there would be no authority behind the instructions in the document. The ring symbolized power and authority to carry out the father's business.

This boy, who had squandered his father's wealth in wild living, is being recommissioned and honored with the trust of his father to go about his father's business once again, telling people what they need to do. And they will have to do it, because he wears the ring on his finger.

The third thing he tells the servants to bring is sandals. In a Jewish household, the only people allowed to wear footwear in the house were the father and his sons. The father was declaring in no uncertain terms that the boy, despite everything he had done, was still his son, entitled to the rights of a son.

This is *The Grace Course*, but what is grace? Let's pause for a minute and take in that scene. A son who has behaved in the worst way imaginable returns. His father, however, restores him simply because he loves him and wants a relationship with him. This is grace: a child utterly bereft of anything throwing himself on the mercy of his father who picks him up, dusts him off, and restores him.

This son who has completely and utterly blown it, who has no right whatsoever to expect anything from his father except what he might be allowed to earn, who doesn't deserve any favor whatsoever, stands there in his rich robe, with his ring of authority and the sandals that mark him out as one of the family. This is grace.

Those of us who have been Christians a while know this story well, and we tend to relate it to the time that we first came to God, gave our lives to Him, and accepted

His free gift of grace. But what about now? Does this part of the story have anything to say to us as we live our Christian lives today, or does it just reflect a one-off moment in the past?

[Do you have an incident from your own experience like the one below from Rich Miller that illustrates such grace?]

When I was a kid, I wanted just about every kind of animal that I saw on TV, but what I wanted most was a horse. I didn't know how much a horse cost, but I knew it was more than I had. So I concocted a plot. One Thursday evening I discovered my Mom's purse with a roll of twenty-dollar bills in it. My Dad had just been paid. I figured they wouldn't miss one of them, so I took a twenty.

The next day I grabbed an envelope and the twenty dollars and went to the woods where I often played. I put the twenty dollars into the envelope and rubbed it in the dirt to make it look like it had been there a while. Then an hour or so later, I rushed home and yelled to my mom, "Hey look! I found twenty dollars in the woods!" My mom said, "Great, you can use that toward your horse." I thought I had committed the crime of the century. But I didn't count on one other factor . . . my conscience. The next day I was playing baseball, and my Dad was watching from a low hill nearby. When I finished playing, I started walking toward him, and the closer I came, the worse I felt. Finally when I got to him, I sort of blubbered, "Dad, I didn't find that money. I stole it!" My dad said, "Son, your mother and I knew that you stole the money. We were just waiting for you to come and tell us." And with that, he hugged me, and I was bawling.

What is the worst thing you have ever done? Have you got it in your head? Okay, write it down on a piece of paper and hand it to the person sitting next to you. . . . Just kidding! But what if you went out of here and did it again or did something even worse . . . and then sincerely came back to God, what reception would you get? The logic of this story is that you would be treated in exactly the same way as this boy.

This is grace. And it genuinely is amazing

Does the thought that you as a Christian could behave in the worst way imaginable and then come back to God with the relationship still secure not sit quite right with you?

> THE CONTEXT OF THE STORY

Let's step back and look at why Jesus told this story in the first place. The context is that He was clearly setting Himself up as a religious teacher but He sure didn't act like one. He was always mixing with the "wrong" crowd, tax collectors and so-called "sinners," and the religious people complained, saying "This man welcomes sinners and even sits down to eat with them." In response Jesus told a series of stories, of which this is the third. So He told it in response to the accusation that His behavior was wrong—that it was displeasing to God. The whole point of the story is that it is not our behavior that puts us into a right relationship with God—it's His grace.

> BUT BEHAVIOR DOES MATTER

As we will see, it's not that the son's behavior did not matter. It did. Sin has consequences. But the ending of his relationship with his father was NOT one of those consequences. That's what it means to be a child of God. You will always be a child of God. Even if you fall flat on your face and make a complete mess. God gives you freedom to fail. He is rooting for you and has given you everything you need so that you do not have to fail. But if you do, His loving arms are there to welcome you back and pick you up no matter how badly you have messed up. This is genuinely shocking, don't you find? But that's exactly what the Bible says in 1 John 2:1:

> My dear children, I write this to you so that you will not sin. But if anybody does sin, we have an advocate with the Father—Jesus Christ, the Righteous One.

There's an old heresy—nearly as old as the gospel itself—called antinomianism which pushes biblical truth too far and says that, since we are saved by God's grace through faith, there is no need for a moral law, so our behavior doesn't matter. If it's starting to sound a little like that's where we're going, let me reassure you that it isn't. If you bear with us, you'll get the full picture.

See the section on antinomianism in the Leader's Notes on page 33 for more information on this.

PAUSE FOR THOUGHT 1

OBJECTIVE

To help people start to come to grips with the shocking concepts of God's grace and particularly their new position as children of God.

1. **What does "grace" mean to you?**

2. **The father gives the younger son three gifts which symbolize things that God has given to you. Which gift is most meaningful to you? Why?**

PART B

> THE ELDER BROTHER

What is the worst thing you ever did? If you did it again or worse . . . and then sincerely came back to God, what reception would you get? The logic of this story is that you would be treated in exactly the same way as the younger son was.

Does that thought—that you could behave in the worst way imaginable and then come back to God with the relationship still intact and secure—not sit quite right with you?

Let's step back and look at why Jesus told this story. He looked like a religious teacher, but He didn't do what the religious people expected. In particular, He was mixing with the "wrong" crowd, and they were saying "This man welcomes sinners and even sits down to eat with them."

Their accusation is that the way Jesus is behaving is plain wrong—and this story is part of Jesus' response.

So now Jesus introduces a character who is often overlooked but is in fact the main point of the story and is clearly meant to represent these religious people.

> "Meanwhile, the older son was in the field. When he came near the house, he heard music and dancing. So he called one of the servants and asked him what was going on. 'Your brother has come,' he replied, 'and your father has killed the fattened calf because he has him back safe and sound.'
>
> "The older brother became angry and refused to go in. So his father went out and pleaded with him. But he answered his father, 'Look! All these years I've been slaving for you and never disobeyed your orders. Yet you never gave me even a young goat so I could celebrate with my friends. But when this son of yours who has squandered your property with prostitutes comes home, you kill the fattened calf for him!'
>
> "'My son,' the father said, 'you are always with me, and everything I have is yours. But we had to celebrate and be glad, because this brother of yours was dead and is alive again; he was lost and is found.'"
>
> Luke 15:25–31

The older brother hadn't turned away from the father and thrown everything back in his face. He had stayed and worked hard. He had done what was expected of him.

It seems his motivation was the inheritance that he would one day receive in return for "slaving away" day after day, as he put it. To him, it was clearly a transaction: You *earn* the father's favor by what you do.

When his brother returned after all he had done and, instead of being turned away or at least severely disciplined, had a party thrown for him, you can almost hear him spluttering, "But, but, but . . . All these years I have done everything right. I've played by the rules. And you never threw a party for me. It's so unfair!"

He didn't understand that the father's love and acceptance was as little to do with his *good* outward behavior as it was with the younger son's *bad* outward behavior. And that's Jesus' point: God's love, acceptance, and favor have nothing to do with our behavior, good or bad. But everything to do with His grace.

The traditional picture is of a rich father taking his son around the estate and saying, "One day son, all this will be yours." Future tense. This father says something similar but different: "Everything I have is yours." Present tense. "Look around you. It's already yours."

And perhaps it dawns on him that instead of working in the fields for years, he could have been enjoying everything the father had. . . . What a tragedy to go through life slaving away to try to earn something that in fact you already have.

Most Christians I know are like this brother. We don't know what we already have—or, more to the point, just who we already are. On one level we know we are saved by grace, not by obeying rules. But we slip into thinking that being a disciple of Jesus means somehow having to *maintain* that favor by doing the right things.

The mind-blowing point of Jesus' story is that God's acceptance of me, of you, today, tomorrow, and every day after that does not depend on what you do or fail to do. It depends solely on His grace.

That's what it means to be a child of God. God gives you freedom to fail. I remember, as a parent, having to let go of my toddler daughter's hand, knowing there's a risk she's going to fall. And she did fall. But even if you fall flat on your face and make a complete mess, God is there to pick you up, dust you off, and welcome you back.

PAUSE FOR THOUGHT 2

OBJECTIVE

To help people recognize how they tend to view God and His reaction to good and bad behavior, and how that works out in their lives.

1. **The younger brother has been received back as a son, but the elder brother refuses to go into the house with the father, preferring to remain in the fields acting like a slave. Why do you think he does that? Which son do you identify with more?**

2. **If you knew for sure that God's acceptance of you and love for you did not depend on how well you behaved, how might that change the way you live?**

PART C

> SLAVING OR SERVING?

The younger son went to a "distant land" whereas the elder brother stayed at home. But Jesus doesn't put him where you would expect to find him, in the home with the father. He's out in the fields. Where, in his own words, he's "slaving away."

The younger son thought the best he could hope for was that the father might just possibly allow him to become a hired servant where he would earn anything that came from the father. But the older son has beaten him to it. That was exactly the identity he had taken on.

Both walked away from their true identity as sons. Both removed themselves from their relationship with their father. Both ended up thinking they had to earn the father's favor.

At the start of our Christian life, most of us identify strongly with the younger son. We know we need forgiveness and salvation and are so grateful to receive them.

At that point we begin a new relationship with our Heavenly Father. And the idea is that we begin a journey of knowing Him and becoming more and more like Him.

But some of us are sidetracked by the world out there and its false promises, and we become like the younger brother.

Others are sidetracked by religious rules and become like the elder brother, thinking that being a Christian, is about doing the "right" things. And most churches have been happy to come up with a whole list of things to do: read your Bible every day; come to church every week. Now those are good things. But when discipleship becomes just a load of rules that we struggle to obey, it all becomes a joyless trudge.

It's supposed to work the other way around. Imagine the younger son after the celebrations are over. As he returns to his old duties—the duties he had thrown off when he walked away—how do you think he feels about those duties? Especially as he now realizes that even if he chooses not to do them, the father will still love him and he will still be his son.

Knowing what he now knows about the father and out of this incredible new relationship with him, won't he choose to do them and do them well? Not because he *has* to but because he *want*s to. Not to earn anything. Just out of love.

WHAT WE DO MATTERS

Paul tells us (1 Corinthians 3:12–15) that a day will come at the end of the age when God tests what we've done to see if it has any real value. What we do does absolutely matter. He uses the analogy of a building that's on fire and says that the fire will burn up the things that are of no value—"wood, hay, straw"—while things we do that are of value—"gold, silver, precious stones"—will remain forever.

Jesus tells us that some will come to Him at the end of time and say they did amazing things like driving out demons and performing miracles in His name. Are those wood, hay, and straw, or gold, silver, and precious stones? Well, Jesus says He will say to them, "'I never knew you. Away from me, you evildoers!'" (Matthew 7:22–23 NIV).

IT'S NOT JUST WHAT WE DO BUT WHY WE DO IT

Two people can do the same thing—feeding the poor, perhaps, or spending an hour a day reading His word and praying. One will delight God and count for eternity; the other will not.

What's the difference?

"If I give away all I have, and if I deliver up my body to be burned, but have not love, I gain nothing" (1 Corinthians 13:3).

If our motivation is not love, then no matter how good our actions look, they are worth precisely nothing. They are wood, hay, and straw. What is important to God is not just what we do but why we do it.

God chose a very unlikely candidate, David, to be king of Israel—unlikely because he was the youngest and smallest in his family. But the Lord told Samuel, "'The LORD sees not as man sees: man looks on the outward appearance, but the LORD looks on the heart" (1 Samuel 16:7).

Jesus said, "If you love me, you will keep my commandments" (John 14:15). I used to picture Him saying that with a stern expression on his face like a strict teacher. Now I know He is smiling, and His eyes are full of love. He's simply explaining a fact. If I love Him, I will obey His commands. I just will. As night follows day.

What's important to God is not just *what* we do but *why* we do it.

1 John 4:19 says, "We love because he first loved us." If we know how much He loves us, we will love Him back. We just will. As night follows day. And that means we'll do the things that please Him. Automatically. Not out of obligation. And that makes understanding grace the most important thing we can do as Christians.

When our understanding and experience of grace makes that long journey from head to heart, we really "get it." It's only then we can be like Paul who said it's "Christ's love [that] compels us" (2 Corinthians 5:14 NIV).

God wants our motivation to be love and nothing but love. It's so easy to be sidetracked and allow our motivation to become something else: shame, guilt, fear, pride, the need to perform and impress or please others.

As you go through *The Grace Course*, you'll have the opportunity to work out what's been motivating you. You'll be able to root out these "false motivators" so that you can make sure that it's love for Jesus that drives you on. And nothing else.

> THE FATHER

The Father is looking out for you. Whether you're in full rebellion or slaving away in the fields. When He sees you, He will run out and embrace you—and call for the robe, the ring, and the sandals. Will you put them on?

When He tells you that all He has is already yours—His whole, vast, rich estate—it's already yours! Will you come back inside the house and enjoy it with Him?

From that position of love and security, will you do the things He has prepared for you to do—even though you don't have to? But just because you love Him? Will you make Jesus not just your Savior, but your King?

REFLECT

Introduction

In our own eyes it's very possible to believe we are doing all the right things, while in God's eyes, we're doing them for all the wrong reasons. God isn't simply concerned about what we do but also why we do it. In our first "Reflect" time, ask God to talk to you about what motivates you to do what you do as a Christian. And remember, He's the God of grace who loves you just as you are!

Reflection

Think about what you are doing to serve God across the whole of your life. Are these things motivated by your love for God or by other things? Ask God to help you understand what needs to change so that your motivation becomes love and nothing but love.

Why do you think God puts so much importance on your motivation being love?

> CONCLUDING THE SESSION

Recommend that participants go to the YouVersion Bible App *right now* and search for "Daily Nuggets Of Grace," the devotional that accompanies this course. If they start it today, they will be able to follow seven short daily devotionals in the coming week that will help them continue to reflect on the themes of this session and prepare them for the next one.

Tell them about *The Wonder Of Grace* introductory videos (if you haven't already) and suggest that they watch the second one to prepare them for the next session.

Show them a copy of *The Grace Connection*, the book that accompanies *The Grace Course*.

If you have a date for an Away Day to go through *The Steps To Experiencing God's Grace*, ensure that participants have it in their calendars.

Close in prayer.

session **02**

UNASHAMED!

OBJECTIVE

To understand that our very identity at the core of our being was comprehensively transformed the moment we came to Christ.

LEADER'S NOTES

In our experience, many Christians understand that their sins are forgiven and that they are going to go to heaven when they die, but they still see themselves as essentially the same no-good person that they always were, just "covered" by the blood of Jesus. They have only got as far as Good Friday in their thinking.

The point of this session is to help them progress to Easter Sunday and understand that it is not just Jesus who rose again to new life; they rose with Him. They have become completely new creations. In fact, as our focus verse makes clear, they have actually become the righteousness of God. An exchange has taken place. Christ became sin for me so that I could become the righteousness of God!

Knowing that we are now fundamentally acceptable to God in our very identity is key to living a righteous life. As Neil Anderson loves to point out, no one can consistently live in a manner that is inconsistent with how they see themselves.

Shame strikes at the heart of our identity and tells us that we are not acceptable. It makes us want to cover up and hide away. As people come out of shame, they are free to be themselves without the need to project an image or hide away. It's a wonderful thing to see people take hold of the truth of their new identity in Christ.

One of the key parts of this session is the list called "My New Name." It can be a very powerful aid in helping participants to understand their true identity in Christ. We recommend that you encourage participants to read it out loud every day in the coming week.

If you have any participants who have not yet made a definite decision to follow Jesus, we would recommend reminding people that these amazing truths apply only to those who are in Christ and remind them of the encouragement made in the previous session to turn to Him in their hearts.

You may be surprised how few understand that the sin of one man, Adam, made all of us sinners. It comes as a new concept to some that they were guilty before God even before they themselves sinned.

For some people, this session will raise the question of what happens to unborn babies that die. Our advice is not to raise this topic yourself because it can lead to long, fruitless discussions but, if it is raised, you can say that the Bible makes no definitive statement on this subject and Christians have come to different views. Most—but not all—end up concluding that, through some mechanism that we don't understand, God is able to save those who are unborn through the sacrifice of Jesus. At the end of the day, however, we do not know the answer. What we do know is that God is love and that He is a God of perfect justice. He will not do anything unjust or unloving. Advise those for whom this is a pertinent issue to focus on God's love and perfect justice and to come to a place where they are able to trust Him to do the right thing.

> ADULT AND TEEN GROOMING

In the video for this session, Nancy Maldonado shares the story of how, as an older teen, she was groomed for a sexual relationship by a married worship leader in her church who carefully built her trust and then abused it.

Grooming happens within churches for two main reasons: firstly, because attenders naturally assume that it is a "safe" place where they can let down their guard; and secondly, because there is an imbalance of power between attendants and leaders.

Spiritual leaders hold a place of authority (power) and are looked up to and even revered (trust). This mix of power and trust can easily be abused.

It is beyond the scope of this course to go into this in more detail, but we do encourage you to become aware of the signs of grooming and to keep your eyes and ears open.

We found an article on www.SkillsPlatform.org/blog helpful. Search for "6 Stages of Grooming Adults and Teens: Spotting The Red Flags."

SMALL GROUP TIMINGS

The following plan is designed to help those leading the course in small groups. It assumes a meeting of around ninety minutes in length, and suggests how long each part of the session should last, with an indication of cumulative elapsed time. You will find a time plan in each session. The second column shows the time allocated to each individual element in minutes and seconds. The third column shows the total elapsed time in hours and minutes.

Session 2	Minutes:Seconds	Hours:Minutes
Welcome, Focus, Connect	15:00	00:15
Word Part A	12:00	00:27
Pause For Thought 1	10:00	00:37
Word Part B	11:00	00:48
Pause For Thought 2	12:00	01:00
Word Part C	12:30	01:12
Reflect	18:00	01:30

The time allocated for the Word sections is based on the length of the corresponding section of the videos. Registered users of the course can download an Excel spreadsheet with these timings. Simply enter your own start time, adjust the length of the various components if desired and you will have a customized plan for your session.

*For our sake he made him to be sin who knew no sin, so that
in him we might become the righteousness of God.*

2 Corinthians 5:21

FOCUS TRUTH

We have not just been covered with the righteousness of Christ. We have actually *become* the righteousness of God.

CONNECT

Tell the group about an embarrassing moment you
have experienced.

Divide into pairs and take it in turns to read Hebrews
10:19–22 (NIV) out loud to each other, inserting the
other person's name:

> Therefore _____ (their name) since you have confidence
> to enter the Most Holy Place by the blood of Jesus," etc.

If you watched *The Wonder Of Grace* introductory
video for this session, what was the main thing that
struck you?

Was there anything in the YouVersion "Daily Nuggets
Of Grace" that especially made you think?

PRAYER & DECLARATION

In every session, we want to encourage people to pray out loud and to make a declaration out loud together. A prayer is addressed to God while a declaration is spoken out to the spiritual world in general.

Encourage people to make their declaration boldly!

Heavenly Father, we welcome Your presence with us right now. Please continue to root out any "false motivators" within us so that it's love for Jesus alone that drives us on as Your children. Please teach us today how Your grace brings us out of disgrace into freedom. Amen.

I DECLARE THE TRUTH THAT I AM NOW A NEW CREATION IN CHRIST; THE OLD HAS GONE AND THE NEW HAS COME! I HAVE BEEN CLEANSED FROM SIN AND NO LONGER HAVE TO HIDE BEHIND MASKS. I COMMAND EVERY ENEMY OF THE LORD JESUS TO LEAVE MY PRESENCE.

○ WORD

PART A

SHAME VERSUS GUILT

Welcome to Session 2 of *The Grace Course* which is called "Unashamed!"

We said last time that we'll have the opportunity to work out what's *motivating* us, so that we can root out "false motivators" and make sure that it's love for Jesus—and nothing but love for Jesus—that drives us on in our Christian life.

Last session we looked at the story Jesus told about a younger brother who messes up massively. He feels such shame that the best he can hope for is to return with his tail between his legs and to be hired as a servant to his father.

How the father in the story actually treats the younger brother is a shock. It's outrageous even. He completely restores him. And the younger son just doesn't see it coming.

I completely understand. I grew up in a low-tech family, so when I went off to Bible college, it was really my first time using the internet. I had never watched an online video. I didn't even know what a blog was. And the first time I stumbled across online pornography, I was completely surprised, shocked. It was 100 percent accidental. The second time, I was less surprised. By the third time I did it, I knew I had a problem. Not only was I getting entangled in sin, I also felt covered with a thick layer of shame. From an outward appearance, my Christian life looked the same. But inwardly, I wanted to hide from God and distance myself from His people.

Shame is the first false motivator we want to deal with. It's not the same thing as guilt—that's another big false motivator that we'll look at in the next session.

Guilt is about what we *do*. But shame is about who we *are*.

Guilt says, "I've *done* something wrong. I *made* a mistake." Shame, on the other hand, says, "There's something wrong with *me*. I *am* the mistake." It strikes at our very identity.

CONSEQUENCES OF ADAM'S SIN

Where did shame and guilt come from? Let's start back at the beginning of time when God's love moved Him to create incredible universes, amazing galaxies, and this wonderful planet.

The Father, the Son, and the Holy Spirit already enjoyed a beautiful loving relationship, and God's great desire was to include others in that. So He created human beings.

He gave us a task: to work with Him to continue bringing order out of chaos as we look after this world.

God didn't make us as robots who had to do what He told us to. Out of love, He gave us the ability to decide for ourselves.

So Adam was totally free to accomplish the mission God had given him in any way he chose. God didn't burden him with rules but said just one thing: He told him not to eat fruit from a certain tree. And He explained why: "'for when you eat from it you will certainly die'" (Genesis 2:17 NIV).

This wasn't some kind of test to see how well Adam behaved. Genuine freedom includes genuine consequences for the choices we make. And, out of love, God wanted Adam to avoid the unpleasant consequences of a bad choice.

But! God's enemy, Satan, deceived Eve. She and Adam chose to disobey God. Like the younger son, they turned their backs on their Father and walked away.

And, just as God had warned, there were huge consequences, not just for them but for their children, their children's children, and all their descendants right down to us.

Adam and Eve did indeed die. Spiritually. They lost their spiritual connection to God and all that came with it: their significance, their intimacy with God, their security. They were cut off from the fellowship with God they had enjoyed.

Their fundamental identity changed. Paul says this to the Romans: "by the one man's disobedience [and he means Adam] the many were made sinners" (Romans 5:19). In the New Testament the word sinner describes those who are spiritually dead, who are disconnected from God.

WHAT IS A "SINNER?"

In the New Testament, the word *sinner* describes those who are spiritually dead, who are disconnected from God. Being a sinner is a condition, a state of being. We didn't *become* sinners the first time we sinned. It's the other way around. We were *born* spiritually dead—disconnected, cut off from the life of God—and therefore our default setting was to do things our way, sinning against God. We were doomed to hurt ourselves, those around us, and pretty much everything we touched.

SHAME MAKES US WANT TO HIDE

Before Adam sinned, Genesis tells us, "The man and his wife were both naked and were not ashamed" (Genesis 2:25). And after?

> The eyes of both of them were opened, and they realized they were naked; so they sewed fig leaves together and made coverings for themselves.
>
> Genesis 3:7 NIV

Right there you have the origin of shame.

The English word *shame* originally meant "covering up." And this horrible feeling of shame that they had never experienced before made them want to do just that. But even with the fig leaves, Adam and Eve still felt exposed and tried to hide from God. As if that were possible!

Shame makes us feel so vulnerable that we want to cover up and hide away from God and other people.

Shame is to do with our identity. That's why it affects us so deeply. We try to cope by hiding, covering up, just hoping it won't happen again, but just like those fig leaves, our coping mechanisms don't work. God's got a far better remedy. It's to give us a whole new identity.

PAUSE FOR THOUGHT 1

OBJECTIVE

To help people realize how shame makes us cover up and hide and to start thinking about the fundamental issue of our identity.

1. **What has God done for you personally out of love? How do those things affect how you view yourself?**

2. **When we feel shame we try to "cover up" and hide away like Adam and Eve did. What are some ways you have seen shame lead people to do that?**

PART B

> SHAME IS INTENSIFIED BY SHAME-BASED CULTURES

Have you ever had an embarrassing moment? You tripped and fell, or you had a wardrobe malfunction, or you forgot someone's name? We all have our moments! And they stay with us forever. The ones we play out in our mind over and over again when we're lying awake in bed at 2 a.m., fighting the thought that the person who witnessed it might still remember it!

How do moments like that make you feel? You want the ground to swallow you up!

Embarrassment is actually a mild form of shame.

Our life experiences tend to determine how much of an issue shame is for us.

It's worse if we were raised in a shame-based culture.

All societies have ways of making us conform to their expectations. Anthropologists will tell you that individualistic Western societies tend to use *guilt* for this, and we'll look at that in the next session.

Other societies, particularly Eastern and African ones, use *shame*. In these more collectivistic cultures, if you don't conform to social norms, you bring dishonor and shame to yourself and to your family.

In a shame-based culture, what matters most is obtaining honor and avoiding shame; being accepted and avoiding rejection by the community. It's not so much a question of whether what you do is wrong or right but whether it meets the expectations of the group.

For the record, we're not saying that either of these cultures are "the good" or "the bad" one. But being brought up in a shame-based culture makes you more susceptible to having shame as a primary motivation.

Some institutions—even Christian ones, or perhaps *especially* Christian ones—can create shame-based subcultures, even in a society that is not shame-based.

For example, church leaders can subtly imply that you should behave in a certain way to be accepted in a church or to be a "good Christian." If we don't measure up, we end up feeling that there's something wrong with *us*. That's shame.

And *parents* can unwittingly create a culture of particular expectations. Maybe these sound familiar:

- *Of course you're going to study well and be a doctor or a missionary. . . .*
- *What a disgrace you are to the family!*
- *No child of mine would do something like that!*

If children feel they don't measure up, it can be devastating.

And the world out there also sets unreachable standards. Take appearance, for example. Look around you at fashion magazines, ads, and movies. Sadly, the dominant standard for women is White European beauty: light skin, slim nose, straight hair, tall, and ridiculously slim.

If we believe the world's lies about beauty, we end up feeling ugly, like there's something wrong with *us*. So we try to "fix" our appearance to fit in and be accepted.

From an early age, we're immersed in all these messages.

> *It's particularly hard for us women of color. You know, I remember as a girl wearing a clothespin on my nose to make it thinner. Because of the texture and length of our natural hair, we women of African descent often use various methods to modify the texture of our hair and spend lots of money on a variety of wigs in order to feel acceptable.*

Women now feel the pressure to become overly obsessed with working out and dieting or get surgery to obtain designer bodies with small waists and more voluptuous body parts. As if what we look like determines our value.

And yet less than 2 percent of the population meet the body standards of actors, models, and influencers. So 98 percent of us are trying to conform to the marginal 2 percent? Let's stop this nonsense!

SHAME IS INTENSIFIED BY PAST EXPERIENCES

We can also be predisposed to feel shame because of things we've done or things other people did to us, particularly in childhood.

Maybe we were abused in some way. Maybe we even feel it was somehow our fault or that we deserved it. But children are never to blame for the shameful acts of perpetrators.

If that's you today, I am very, very sorry that you suffered so terribly. And so is Jesus, the one who came specifically to bind your broken heart and set you free.

> *I was a victim of sexual abuse as an older teen. Until then I'd never had a boyfriend because I was waiting for a godly relationship when the time was right. But my worship team leader, who was married, abused his position and seduced me. And because sexual grooming is based on a web of deceit, I was blind to the tangle of sin I was trapped in.*

> *When I was found out, my dad confronted me with truth and in love. That's when the blinders fell, and I was devastated. I couldn't recognize myself. I couldn't believe what I was capable of. I had fallen very low and had betrayed everyone I loved. Shame covered me like a thick cloud.*

> *My marriage didn't work out, and so I'm now divorced. When I became a Christian and went to church, my pastor told me not to let anyone at church know about it. It made me feel there was something wrong with me—that was shame. I then saw that divorced persons often were sidelined and even prevented from doing ministry in some churches. When asked about my marital status, I would say I am not married rather than say I am divorced. I felt like the girl with the scarlet letter. Often people will give me the "oh" when I tell them that I'm divorced and then the "look" when I tell them I am unmarried and have no children, as if there must* definitely *be something wrong with me.*

THE "LESS MESS"

Yes, shame's basic message is that there's something wrong with **us**, that **we** are the problem. It puts us into what we call the "less mess." We feel help*less*, worth*less*, meaning*less*, power*less*, hope*less*. So we hide, we wear masks, we avoid, we pretend. And we never feel truly accepted.

In our shame, there are all sorts of ways we cover up and try to hide.

There's lying. I was tempted to give the impression I wasn't divorced.

Or blame-shifting by making everyone else appear to be the problem rather than us. If I don't feel OK, nothing around me feels OK, so, everyone, go fix it!

Or we pretend everything's okay and we're doing great when we know we're not. Something I've done many times—putting on a show, while silently dying inside.

Criticizing others harshly in order to make them appear inferior to us. If I feel rejected, I'm tempted to reject back.

Compromising moral or biblical values to fit in and avoid the shame of rejection.

Self-medicating in order to numb the pain of our own shame. For me it was parties and alcohol.

Striving for perfection in our behavior or our looks to compensate for that painful belief that in reality we fall far short of who we should be.

All these defense mechanisms are like Adam and Eve's fig leaves; they don't quite work to cover our shame. Remember, they continued to hide even *after* covering themselves with DIY fig-leaf underwear. They may offer some relief, but in the end, like all strategies of the flesh, they fail. God has a better way!

PAUSE FOR THOUGHT 2

OBJECTIVE

To help people understand how shame-based cultures have influenced their thinking.

Note that Christians can experience mini shame-based cultures, for example in their home or church, even if they don't live in a wider shame-based culture.

1. Has any person or any culture you have experienced used shame to try to make you behave in a certain way? How has it affected you?

2. What would God say to you about situations where you felt shame?

PART C

THE GREAT EXCHANGE

When the younger son returned to his father he said: "'I am no longer worthy to be called your son; make me like one of your hired servants'" (Luke 15:19 NIV). Remember, shame strikes at our very identity. He no longer saw himself as a son but had taken on the identity of a servant—someone who would be accepted only based on performance.

Shame makes him consider himself *unworthy* of being a son. He's willing to take on the identity of a servant—someone worth only as much as his work.

I felt like that the day our school principal brought me home and told my parents that I had been blatantly disrespectful to my teacher. The consequences were painful, including hours in the school boiler room, a project for summer break, and a week without seeing any friends.

Like the younger brother's father, my own father helped me understand that, despite all that I had done, I was still his son. Both of us were embraced, welcomed, and accepted back. Our bad behavior did not affect our true identity as sons.

OUR OLD IDENTITY

What about you? What's your identity? As we've seen, we were all born spiritually dead—disconnected from God. Paul tells us that we *were* "by nature children of wrath" (Ephesians 2:3). He speaks in the past tense. We were not the people God intended us to be. And there was nothing we could do about it.

OUR NEW IDENTITY

And he says this too: "While we *were* [past tense] still sinners, Christ died for us" (Romans 5:8). The New Testament uses the word *sinner* to describe those who are not Christians. And Paul makes clear that that's not who we are any more.

2 Corinthians 5:21 reveals why: "For our sake he made him to *be* sin who knew no sin, so that in him we might *become* the righteousness of God."

On the cross, Jesus, who was totally blameless, *became* sin for our sake. God took all our shortcomings, failures, rebellion, and shame and laid them on Christ. He didn't die just to pay the penalty for our sin. He also took on Himself our defiled, unclean nature and destroyed our inner contamination. And then He rose from the dead to new life.

When we surrender our life to Jesus, this great exchange takes place. We don't just get our sins forgiven. A clean slate is great, but it's deeper than that. We actually *become* someone very different. We *become* the righteousness of God.

Ezekiel's amazing prophecy is fulfilled: we get a new heart and a new spirit (see Ezekiel 11:19). We're no longer *by nature* objects of wrath because we now share God's *divine nature* (see 2 Peter 1:4). Just think about that! What was wrong with us died! The shame of who we used to be is gone!

In short, we've become a whole new person. We now have a totally new, clean, wonderful identity. And instead of calling us "sinners," the Bible's standard phrase for those who are in Christ is *holy ones*. In some translations, Paul addresses his letters, for example, to "the holy ones in Ephesus" or to "the holy ones in Corinth."

Yes, you are now a holy one. *Holy* means set apart for God. Special. Like a wedding dress that you don't wear on any old day. It's set apart for one special purpose. Deep in the core of your being, your very identity has changed. From someone disconnected, cut off from God, to someone who is accepted, significant, and secure in Christ.

Our shame has been completely taken away. Once and for all. Past, present, and future! You're not contaminated any more. You're not unacceptable. You're clean. You're presentable. You can take off your mask and let down the walls. You *can* show yourself to God and to others with no shame whatsoever!

In the midst of my shame with pornography, I hated myself. But when I opened the New Testament again, I was completely awestruck by how unconditional God's love for me is, and by how completely clean He had made me—even though I didn't feel clean or pure. I realized my identity was not that of a sinner—in spite of being stuck in a sin. God had made me holy, and in looking at pornography I was acting out of character. Knowing my new identity in Christ gave me the courage to share my struggle with others, who helped me overcome that sin—that way my actions caught up with my identity as a holy one.

And here's God's invitation to you:

Since we have confidence to enter the holy places by the blood of Jesus, by the new and living way that he opened for us through the curtain, that is, through his flesh, and since we have a great high priest over the house of God, let us draw near with a true heart in full assurance of faith, with our hearts sprinkled clean from an evil conscience and our bodies washed with pure water. (Hebrews 10:19–22)

After the relationship with my worship leader was exposed, my dad walked me through a healing process. With the insight of his therapist colleagues they identified it as a grooming situation.

Which did not exempt me from my responsibility, but helped us understand how we had all been blindsided—me, my dad, the worship team, the pastors.

Through that painful experience I learned the truth about myself and about God. Believing I was "good" had blinded me to my inclination toward rebellion and sin. A "good" girl doesn't need a savior! Finally I understood that I was capable of anything, given the right circumstances, just like everyone else. I, too, needed to be rescued from darkness into God's marvelous light.

But I also understood that just as Christ did not accept me for being "good," He did not reject me for being "bad." I could leave behind self-righteousness and haughtiness, but I didn't have to pick up shame.

We don't have to run away any more. We don't have to hide, no matter what's in our past, or even in our present, because we have a new, clean identity in Christ. We're invited to come near to God in the Holy of Holies. Because we *are* holy ones!

OUR NEW NAME

In Isaiah 62:2 we read:

> The nations shall see your righteousness, and all the kings your glory, and you shall be called by a new name that the mouth of the LORD will give.

Did you know that God has given you a new name? Many of them in fact. In your notes, there is a list from the Bible of your new names. Every one of them describes you and me, even if they don't *feel* true right now.

After the session, read them out loud and ask God to plant one of these new names deep in your heart.

For me, it's been important to know that I am clean. I *am* forgiven. I *am* free from condemnation. I *am* pure. This

reality raised me out of my pit of sin and shame. It gave me hope that God not only loved me,0 but liked me. That He still had a plan for me and still wanted to use me to bring change to this world. It gave me an anchor for my soul, which did not depend on me being good enough, but was built entirely on His grace.

All my life I longed to feel precious —a longing that is now fulfilled because I now know I'm valuable to God, not just another sheep among many. I rest knowing I'm protected—because I tend to feel alone and vulnerable in scary and painful situations. Being a mom also helped me understand I'm God's delight; as his daughter, God doesn't just tolerate me, He delights in me, like I delight in my children, just because they're mine!

What about you? In the Bible, names were much more than labels. They were seen as a reflection of the person's identity. For example, Peter means "rock" on whom Jesus would build His church.

These new names are truths about you. At the deepest level of your being. Because of God's grace.

The question we all face is: Am I going to believe what God says about me in His Word? Or am I going to believe what my past experiences, my present struggles, or other people tell me? The choice is yours.

Let's allow God's grace to bring us out of disgrace.

Let's learn to live as the holy ones we are!

REFLECT

Introduction

Take a good look through that amazing list of your new names. Read it out loud if you can. Allow the Holy Spirit to impress upon you one or more names that He wants you to take hold of.

Reflection

Write down the "new name(s)" that particularly strike a chord with you. Thank God for who you now are.

Sharing with someone else helps to move this truth from the head to the heart. At an appropriate moment, turn to your neighbor and share with each other your new names. Who else can you share your new name with in the coming week?

> CONCLUDING THE SESSION

Remind participants about "Daily Nuggets Of Grace," the devotional that accompanies this course that can be accessed on the YouVersion Bible App, *The Wonder Of Grace* introductory videos, and *The Grace Connection*, the book that accompanies *The Grace Course*.

If you have a date for an Away Day to go through *The Steps To Experiencing God's Grace*, ensure that participants have it in their calendars.

Close in prayer.

> MY NEW NAME

My new name is **Beloved** (Colossians 3:12)

My new name is **Chosen** (Ephesians 1:4)

My new name is **Precious** (Isaiah 43:4)

My new name is **Loved** (1 John 4:10)

My new name is **Clean** (John 15:3)

My new name is **Presentable** (Luke 17:14)

My new name is **Protected** (Psalm 91:14, John 17:15)

My new name is **Welcomed** (Ephesians 3:12)

My new name is **Heir** (Romans 8:17, Galatians 3:29)

My new name is **Complete** (Colossians 2:10)

My new name is **Holy** (Hebrews 10:10, Ephesians 1:4)

My new name is **Forgiven** (Psalm 103:3, Colossians 2:13)

My new name is **Adopted** (Ephesians 1:5)

My new name is **Delight** (Psalm 147:11)

My new name is **Unashamed** (Romans 10:11)

My new name is **Known** (Psalm 139:1)

My new name is **Planned** (Ephesians 1:11–12)

My new name is **Gifted** (2 Timothy 1:6, 1 Corinthians 12:11)

My new name is **Enriched** (2 Corinthians 8:9)

My new name is **Provided For** (1 Timothy 6:17)

My new name is **Treasured** (Deuteronomy 7:6)

My new name is **Pure** (1 Corinthians 6:11)

My new name is **Established** (Romans 16:25)

My new name is **God's Work of Art** (Ephesians 2:10)

My new name is **Helped** (Hebrews 13:5)

My new name is **Free from Condemnation** (Romans 8:1)

My new name is **God's Child** (Romans 8:15)

My new name is **Christ's Friend** (John 15:15)

My new name is **Christ's Precious Bride** (Isaiah 54:5, Song of Songs 7:10).

FREEDOM IN CHRIST

session **03**

INNOCENT!

OBJECTIVE

To understand that our guilt before God was completely dealt with at the cross, that any guilt feelings that remain are not based on reality, and that God uses grace rather than guilt to motivate us to live a holy life.

LEADER'S NOTES

It may at first glance seem that we are downplaying the importance of the gospel message that most of us were brought up on, that Jesus died for our sins. Our intention, however, is to help people develop a more rounded understanding of the gospel, and specifically to help them understand that forgiveness of sins was not the only thing—or even the main thing—that Jesus accomplished. His gifts of new life and a whole new identity are at least as fundamental to us as forgiveness for our sins. Focusing overmuch on one aspect of what Jesus accomplished leads us to overlook other key elements. If we see what He did for us primarily through the lens of sin, guilt, and wrath, it can lead us to develop a distorted understanding of God's character and our new identity.

God's Word is very clear that we were guilty and that Jesus did die to forgive our sins. In no way are we attempting to dispute that. The point we're trying to make is that, when Jesus and Paul and the Biblical writers explained the good news, guilt and forgiveness were not the focus of their explanations.

We also mention the historic focus that the Church has had on guilt and how it acted as a "police officer for the state." We are well aware that, in an attempt to condense hundreds of years of Church history into a couple of sentences, we have ended up making a sweeping generalisation. Of course, there were many parts of the Church that stayed true to the gospel and many Christians paid for that with their lives. If you think it would help your group to add a few balancing sentences of your own, please do so.

Most Christians struggle with some level of guilt feelings that they no longer need to carry. Our prayer is that participants should leave this session having put that struggle to rest once and for all.

SMALL GROUP TIMINGS

The following plan is designed to help those leading the course in small groups. It assumes a meeting of around ninety minutes in length, and suggests how long each part of the session should last, with an indication of cumulative elapsed time. You will find a time plan in each session. The second column shows the time allocated to each individual element in minutes and seconds. The third column shows the total elapsed time in hours and minutes.

Session 3	Minutes:Seconds	Hours:Minutes
Welcome, Focus, Connect	15:00	00:15
Word Part A	10:00	00:25
Pause For Thought 1	14:00	00:39
Word Part B	10:45	00:49
Pause For Thought 2	14:00	01:03
Word Part C	12:15	01:16
Reflect	14:00	01:30

The time allocated for the Word sections is based on the length of the corresponding section of the videos. Registered users of the course can download an Excel spreadsheet with these timings. Simply enter your own start time, adjust the length of the various components if desired and you will have a customized plan for your session.

FOCUS VERSE

And when you were dead in your wrongdoings and the uncircumcision of your flesh, He made you alive together with Him, having forgiven us all our wrongdoings, having canceled the certificate of debt consisting of decrees against us, which was hostile to us; and He has taken it out of the way, having nailed it to the cross.

Colossians 2:13–14 NASB

FOCUS TRUTH

No matter what we have done (even as Christians) and no matter how guilty we may feel, the truth is that our guilt has been completely and utterly paid for by Christ's death on the cross so that we can stand confidently before God, who is pure and holy.

CONNECT

Which road sign would best describe where you are on your journey with God right now? (e.g., stop, steep gradient, diversion/detour, crossroads).

How do you think God would introduce you to me based on your new identity? (For ideas, look back at your new names at the end of Session 2.)

If you watched *The Wonder Of Grace* introductory video for this session, what was the main thing that struck you?

Was there anything in the YouVersion "Daily Nuggets Of Grace" that especially made you think?

PRAYER & DECLARATION

In every session, we want to encourage people to pray out loud and to make a declaration out loud together. A prayer is addressed to God while a declaration is spoken out to the spiritual world in general.

Encourage people to make their declaration boldly!

Heavenly Father, thank You that because I have chosen to make Jesus my King, I have received His free gift of life. Thank You that, in Him, all of Your expectations of me are met in full, meaning I don't need to try harder, prove anything, or compare myself to others. Please help me understand that, even when I go wrong, Jesus' full and complete sacrifice for me remains effective. I'm still forgiven. My guilt is gone. Forever. Amen.

IN CHRIST, I AM FORGIVEN AND DECLARED INNOCENT OF ALL THE CHARGES THAT WERE STACKED AGAINST ME. SO BY THE AUTHORITY OF THE LORD JESUS CHRIST I COMMAND ANY ACCUSING AND CONDEMNING THOUGHTS IN MY MIND TO GO NOW.

WORD

PART A

HOLY ONES

Hello and welcome to our third session, "*Innocent*!"

I distinctly remember the first time I heard that I am now a holy one. It did not sit well with me at all. I thought it was correct and even necessary for us Christians to identify ourselves as sinners because it was real and honest and would keep us humble. I believed that remembering we were sinners kept us aware of our weakness and thus less likely to sin again.

How wrong I was. Now I know that if you identify yourself as a sinner, well, what do sinners do by definition? They sin! To have any hope of living a godly life as a disciple of Jesus, we have to know the truth that we are holy ones.

We can also get the wrong end of the stick when it comes to understanding what God is really like. Getting that straight is key to dealing with the false motivator we want to consider next: guilt.

GOD AND GUILT

Many of us grew up in guilt-based societies and have learned to do what others want us to do simply to avoid feeling guilty. What if you were asked to write the ending to the story of the two brothers starting at the point where the younger brother returns home and asks the father to receive him back as a hired laborer—would you portray the father differently from the way Jesus did?

I certainly would. Shouldn't he expect the son to be thorough in his apology? Shouldn't the son be made aware of how he offended the father and abandoned the family? Shouldn't the son have to prove himself for a time to earn trust and only then be allowed to spend money again?

Your response will depend on how you see God. I know I believed that, as a Christian, I barely made it in and I had to try really hard to please God who I thought was watching me with an eagle eye. I didn't want to disappoint Him or make Him think He made a mistake in choosing me. I didn't want to feel guilty. And so I would set out to do everything perfectly, serving in as many areas as I possibly could—leading youth ministry, being in dance ministry, helping with Bible study, planning church events, being present at all prayer meetings and any other meetings—basically saying yes to any job I was asked to do. If I felt I failed Him, I would beat myself up.

Some of us worry: maybe I don't pray enough; I failed to read the Bible in one year, again; I'm a flop at sharing my faith; I don't have the spiritual gifts she does; I don't seem to hear from God like him; I'm not as fruitful as her, or any number of other things.

I didn't think I could ever measure up to how God wanted me to be. Which condemned me to either walking away, forever resolving to try harder tomorrow, or just being resigned to remain a second-class Christian. I chose the last option.

That's not how God wants us to live. And it's not how God wants us to understand what He is like.

WHY JESUS CAME

Let's step back and ask ourselves: Why did God send Jesus, His only Son, to die for us? Well, what do you think? Why did Jesus come?

For most of my Christian life, I'd have said, "to forgive my sins." And that is, of course, true. But it's interesting if you look at what the Bible actually says. Let's look at three direct quotes from Jesus Himself:

In Luke 19:10 (NIV) Jesus says: **"For the Son of Man came . . . to seek and to save what was lost."**

God is love. In His love, God was moved to pursue and rescue us who were lost. Not to have us burn ourselves out trying to please Him.

In John 10:10 (NIV) Jesus says, **"I have come . . . that they may have life, and have it to the full."**

Adam lost *life*. Jesus came specifically to give that life back. By reconnecting us to God in order to make us holy ones.

In Matthew 20:28 (NIV) Jesus explained, **"The Son of Man did not come to be served, but to serve, and to give his life as a ransom for many."**

A ransom is what was paid to buy someone out of slavery. Jesus gave His life to buy you out of slavery. Slavery to death, to the flesh, to sin, and to Satan.

I hope you're getting the idea. In three different verses where Jesus is explaining specifically why He came, He doesn't even mention that He came to forgive our sins. So, let's try the verses from John that we use the most in our gospel presentations:

"For God so loved the world that he gave his one and only Son, that whoever believes in him shall not perish but have eternal life. For God did not send his Son into the world to condemn the world, but to save the world through him." (John 3:16–17 NIV)

No mention of sins or guilt or forgiveness. It's about *life* again. In fact John makes it clear that God did *not* send Jesus to condemn the world but to save it.

To be very clear, we are not at all saying that we weren't guilty and that Jesus didn't die for our sins. It's clear that we *were* guilty. And Jesus *did* die to forgive our sins. The point we're trying to make is that, when Jesus and Paul and the Biblical writers explained the good news, guilt and forgiveness were *not* the focus of their explanations. So why does guilt loom so large over most of us?

THE CHURCH'S HISTORIC FOCUS ON GUILT

It's a historic and cultural issue. In many so-called Christian countries, the Church and the State became so intertwined that they were practically the same thing. It's one thing to threaten citizens with jail or a whipping when they don't obey the rules. But it's so much more effective if you can threaten them with an eternity in hell! The Church was very happy to act as a kind of police officer for the state. For centuries it warned the populace that God was watching closely and keeping tabs. It went so far as to sell forgiveness for other people. It sounds silly today, but in those times, who wouldn't pay to spare their deceased mother from the eternal flames of hell?

This was at best a distortion of the Biblical gospel message. And at worst, it was a disgraceful and cynical manipulation in the name of Christianity.

But the result is that the concept of guilt and punishment and earning our way into God's good books by our behavior took center stage in our understanding of God and the gospel, and for many of us they remain there to this day.

And that's why, even though we know on one level that we're saved by grace alone through faith, when it comes to living as disciples day by day, many of us are followed around by that cloud of guilt or that nagging feeling that we're not doing enough or not doing it quite right.

And when it comes to those outside, instead of welcoming everybody as God does, the Church often comes across as condemning people for their behavior: for the way they dress, for the way they vote, for the issues they support . . . Yes, we have convinced people that our God is a nitpicking, strict, and hard-to-please grouch. Because that's how we've seen Him. And we, His people, come across as a bunch of killjoys focused on sin, condemnation, and judgment. And that is *not* good news.

PAUSE FOR THOUGHT 1

OBJECTIVE

To help people get a wider understanding of cultures that use guilt to enforce conformity and of the fact that Jesus' coming was about more than dealing with guilt.

1. Has any person or any culture you have experienced used guilt to try to make you behave in a certain way? How has it affected you?

2. In what ways do the reasons Jesus gave for His coming—"Life," "Saved," and "Ransomed"—give you a bigger perspective? How would you explain succinctly to someone else why Jesus came?

PART B

GOD IS LOVE

Let's go back to the story of Adam and Eve after their rebellion and its dreadful consequences. And by the way, you'd be hard pressed to find a theme of guilt and forgiveness there, either. Yes, Adam sinned and all of us have sinned. But the primary consequence of that sin was spiritual death, not anger and condemnation from God.

As the story continues, God doesn't come across as some kind of angry figure who feels wronged and in anger turns His back on the people He created. No, He didn't leave Adam with a feeble fig leaf. He provided clothes for Adam and Eve. And right away God put into motion a plan to restore us, even though He knew it would lead to the death of His Son.

God is love. And His heart is not to condemn but to make things right.

Again to be clear, we're not saying that we weren't guilty before God. We were.

FACT NOT FEELING

So what about your own personal cloud of guilt? Here's the key question: Are you guilty before God?

It helps to be clear about what guilt actually is. It's a legal concept used in the context of a courtroom. A judge or jury, after hearing the facts of the case, comes to a decision that the charge against the defendant is true and pronounces that person guilty. Guilt is a *fact,* not a feeling.

In America, a driver is allowed to turn a corner even if the traffic light is red, as long as no other vehicles are coming. So imagine my frustration, when I did exactly as I had been taught in driving school, no other vehicles were approaching, and I turned the corner though the light was red . . . and I was immediately pulled over by a police officer standing there. The problem was that I was in Uganda, not America. And in Uganda, this is against the law. I didn't feel guilty at all. But that didn't matter. The fact is I had broken the law, so I was guilty. And I was fined as a result.

It's interesting that guilt often leads to a financial penalty. The concepts of guilt and debt are strongly associated. In some languages, such as German, the same word is used for both. And when you say the Lord's prayer, you may say "Forgive us our sins" or "forgive us our trespasses" but the Greek word's core meaning is "debts."

In New Testament times, if someone borrowed money from someone else, a legal document was drawn up itemizing exactly what was owed to whom, what the repayment terms were, and what the consequences for default would be. It was called a certificate of debt. If you have a mortgage, you probably get sent the modern equivalent once a year.

If someone couldn't repay the debt, their property was seized and sold, or they themselves could be taken into slavery.

Colossians 2:13–14 (NASB) says: "And when you were dead in your wrongdoings and the uncircumcision of your flesh, He made you alive together with Him, having forgiven us all our wrongdoings, having canceled the certificate of debt consisting of decrees against us, which was hostile to us; and He has taken it out of the way, having nailed it to the cross."

The USA has a national debt of around 33 trillion dollars and a population of around 330 million. That's a debt of $100,000 for every American citizen. Imagine a baby born today. Through no fault of its own but just by being born American and because of the spending of previous generations, it immediately has a debt of $100,000!

Because of Adam's rebellion, we were all born with a certificate of debt to God. That is to say, we were guilty before God even as we took our first breath. Our subsequent sins increased that debt. And we had no way to pay it. But those verses tell us that God did two significant things. First He made us *alive* with Christ, and gave us that incredible new identity. Then God wrote *"paid in full"* across our certificate of debt, which He nailed to the cross with Jesus.

How many of our sins have been forgiven, according to this passage? All of them! Past, present, and future.

So how much guilt do we still have for our sins? None. Absolutely none! We are totally debt free!

As Paul says: "There is therefore now no condemnation for those who are in Christ Jesus" (Romans 8:1). Now means now, and no means no!

God has forgotten our sins, in the sense that He will never raise these issues and use them against us again. The best a human court can do is declare us "not guilty." God's grace goes further than that. As far as God is concerned, it's as if what you and I did never took place. He declares us "innocent!" And that's a legal fact.

I have a daughter who is very sensitive emotionally—that's how God made her. When she's done something wrong and is confronted, she gets really upset, even if she is not punished. My response to her is "it's over, it's done. It's no longer an issue to me." But she will often come back to me a second or third time to apologize for what she did. Are you like that with God?

In Christ, all of God's expectations of you have been met in full. You don't need to try harder or compare yourself to others. You have nothing to prove, no debt to pay off. Your guilt is gone. Forever. You are innocent! It's a fact!

And if you still *feel* guilty? Then your feelings are lying to you.

Either your conscience has not yet fully grasped the wonder of Christ's total forgiveness, or you're inadvertently listening to the whisper of your enemy, Satan. In either case, the answer is to make a choice to believe what God tells you clearly in His Word is true. You are innocent!

PAUSE FOR THOUGHT 2

OBJECTIVE

To help people distinguish between true guilt and guilt feelings and understand that our true guilt has been dealt with once and for all by Christ.

1. **Can you think of a time when you or someone else did something wrong, but did not *feel* guilty, or conversely felt guilty for something that was not actually wrong?**

2. **Share with the group what the word *debt* brings to mind. Have you ever had a debt you could not pay?**

3. **What do you feel about being declared "innocent" by God Himself?**

PART C

CAN WE KEEP ON SINNING?

So, yes! We are innocent! Does that mean we'll live perfect lives? I wish.

But when we do go wrong, it doesn't change God's love for us. And it doesn't change our identity as holy ones. We can come running back to our Father, and we will always be received with love. We're still the son.

"Hang on a minute!" You may be saying, "If God just accepts us back with no questions asked, doesn't that mean we can just do whatever we like?"

That's an important question. Among the seven letters to churches in Revelation, there is just one, the church in Thyatira, that is commended for its love. But they seem to think that grace means you can do whatever you like, and they're allowing sexual immorality and idol worship.

Jesus' words about the consequences of this, for the ringleader, make for uncomfortable reading:

"Behold, I will throw her onto a sickbed, and those who commit adultery with her, I will throw into great tribulation, unless they repent of her works, and I will strike her children dead." (Revelation 2:22–23)

This is Jesus speaking! Maybe you can't conceive that He would use this kind of language. And it's tempting to skip over verses like this. But think about it. God is love. Therefore, everything He does, and everything He says, must come from love.

Out of love God has laid down boundaries in order to *protect* us. He told Adam not to eat from the tree because He knew the consequences. And it's because God *loves* this lady and this church that He tells her not to continue sinning. His intent is that they will *not* suffer, will *not* die. When we truly understand the consequences of sin, we'll also understand why God takes it so seriously.

If I see one of my kids up a tree moving along a branch that I know is going to break, what should I do? I'm going to start shouting and running towards them. To my child

I'm going to look and sound angry. But actually, I'm expressing love, and any parent would do the same.

John helps us understand more:

> This is the message we have heard from him and proclaim to you, that God is light, and in him is no darkness at all. If we say we have fellowship with him while we walk in darkness, we lie and do not practice the truth. But if we walk in the light, as he is in the light, we have fellowship with one another, and the blood of Jesus his Son cleanses us from all sin. If we say we have no sin, we deceive ourselves, and the truth is not in us. If we confess our sins, he is faithful and just to forgive us our sins and to cleanse us from all unrighteousness. (1 John 1:5–9)

If someone persists in sin and is really not bothered by it, I would have serious questions about whether they actually know Jesus at all. If we are walking openly with our Father, we will *want* to live in the light.

WHEN WE GO WRONG

However, even then our flesh will keep pulling us toward sin. And if we say we don't ever fall for it, we're deceiving ourselves.

But this passage gives a way forward when we go wrong. When we know that God is not angry with us, but still loves us just as much as before, we can agree with God that we have sinned—that's what "confessing" means. But we can also agree with Him that we are completely forgiven in Christ.

Confession is part of what James calls submitting to God. But he tells us not only to submit to God but also to "resist the devil" (James 4:7). The biggest issue with sin is that it opens a great big door of influence to the enemy in our lives that will stop us being fruitful. We need to close that door by submitting *and* resisting.

If you know Freedom In Christ, you'll be aware of *The Steps To Freedom In Christ*, which is a kind, gentle way to do this. At the end of *The Grace Course*, you'll have an opportunity to go through *The Steps To Experiencing God's Grace*, a similar process where you can deal with barriers to grace in your life. There's more about these in your notes, and we'll tell you more as we go through the course.

I really love my kids. But I've found it tough keeping my cool at times, and I could find myself overreacting in anger with precious little love, joy, peace, patience, or even kindness as I told them off.

Afterward I would feel terrible as a dad and far from God. My default response would be to feel sorry for myself, wallow for a bit, make some excuses, say sorry, and then maybe eventually string together enough "quiet times" to earn my way back to feeling good enough about myself and my relationship with God. Just in time to do it again.

But if I respond appropriately, in repentance, if I close that door to the enemy through submitting *and* resisting, God immediately cleanses me from *all* evil and unrighteousness. And I'm restored to an intimacy with Jesus, and with others.

GOD DOES NOT WANT US TO FEEL GUILTY

Is there any place for using guilt as a motivator, perhaps to encourage me not to go wrong again or to help others not to sin? Let's see how Paul approached a whole heap of sin issues in the Corinthian church. They were a bit of a mess—there was jealousy, quarreling, sexual immorality, drunkenness, and class discrimination to name but a few of their issues.

Paul didn't say, "Well we believe in grace so it's okay, it doesn't really matter." Because it did matter. Paul agonized over it because he understood the serious consequences of sin. In the end, he decided to write them a tough letter. The strategy worked, and in a subsequent letter he said this:

I . . . rejoice, not that you were made sorrowful, but that you were made sorrowful to the point of repentance. . . .

For the sorrow that is according to the will of God produces a repentance without regret, leading to salvation, but the sorrow of the world produces death. (2 Corinthians 7:9–10 NASB)

The way I used to respond to falling short as a Dad was "worldly sorrow," a self-destructive cycle of sin and guilt.

Same for me when I was caught in pornography, I was filled with remorse. I beat myself up with guilt. Worldly sorrow is also what Judas experienced after he had betrayed Jesus—he found himself filled with remorse but with no hope. Instead of trusting in the one who was going to the cross for him, he turned away and hanged himself.

GODLY SORROW

But Paul's aim was not to make the Corinthians feel guilty. He wanted them to experience "Godly sorrow" that would lead to repentance without regret.

Look at how Jesus came to Peter. Peter had betrayed his best friend in His greatest hour of need by denying Him three times. When Jesus catches up with him after His resurrection, He doesn't even mention this monumental failure.

He cooks him breakfast and asks him gently three times if he loves Him—once for each of his previous denials. Then Jesus restores him. And this grace meant that Peter was able to experience godly sorrow—"a repentance without regret"—and could move forward.

And as I realized that God's love for me really was unconditional, and how completely clean He had made me, that's what I experienced, too. It still amazes me that, despite all my failures, I am totally innocent before God.

You are, too. God does want you to understand that all sin has consequences, but He doesn't want you to be weighed down with guilt, no matter what you've done, or what you're caught in right now. He wants that sense of Godly sorrow to pull you into His arms, where you will find the same welcome the younger son received.

GRACE—THE MOST POWERFUL MOTIVATOR

So **can** you do whatever you want? If you're asking that question, you're missing the point. When you truly "get" grace, you won't for a minute want to use it as an excuse to keep sinning.

It's *grace, not guilt, that*'s the most powerful motivator to live a righteous life. And in our next session, we're going to see that Jesus died to set us free, not just from the *consequences* of sin, but also from the *power* of sin in our lives.

REFLECT

Introduction

God is love. And when you are love, you can only love. But our finite human minds don't always see His love for what it is. In this time, we are going to ask God to help us understand at a deeper level what this means in practice.

Reflection

Ask God to show you things that you have experienced that have caused you to doubt that He is love. Write them down. Bring them to Him in prayer. Then ask Him to help you begin to understand how He has remained true to His fundamental character of love in those situations.

> CONCLUDING THE SESSION

Remind participants about "Daily Nuggets Of Grace," the devotional that accompanies this course that can be accessed on the YouVersion Bible App, *The Wonder Of Grace* introductory videos, and *The Grace Connection*, the book that accompanies *The Grace Course*.

If you have a date for an Away Day to go through *The Steps To Experiencing God's Grace*, ensure that participants have it in their calendars.

Close in prayer.

FREEDOM
IN CHRIST

session **04**

VICTORIOUS!

OBJECTIVE

To help us understand why our new identity in Christ means that, even though we will sin from time to time, at any given moment we can choose not to, and can put an end to sin-confess cycles.

LEADER'S NOTES

A key theme of *The Grace Course* is helping us see reality as it actually is, that is to say, how God says it is in His Word. The following notes may be helpful as you lead this session.

All of us have been taught to see reality in a particular way, shaped by our culture, our education, our friends, and so on. All of us have a worldview that we believe reflects reality. But actually, none of us see the world perfectly as it really is. All of us are filtering reality through our worldview. And this has a huge effect on our lives.

Many people's worldviews have been conditioned by a belief system—a worldview—that says that our lives are controlled by a kind of universal power that runs through everything—animal, vegetable, and mineral—and by spirits of many types. It's called *animism*, and you can find it all over the world, but it is most prevalent outside the West.

Others of us have been brought up with a worldview conditioned by Western rationalism. That has taught us to look at reality as though it is simply what you can see, touch, and test. It influences us to believe that there is no spiritual reality or, if there is, it has no real relevance to our daily lives.

What you believe about the world determines how you behave. For example, if someone with an animistic worldview were to experience an illness with no obvious physical cause, they are likely to turn to a shaman, someone they believe is an expert in controlling the spiritual powers, to get a remedy. Someone with a Western worldview, on the other hand, wouldn't consult a shaman. They would turn to a medical doctor. And that would be true of most Christians, too, even though James 5 has some very clear instructions that we should turn to Christian leaders in the first instance. (We are not, of course, saying you should not also turn to a medical doctor—see *Keys To Health, Wholeness & Fruitfulness,* a course for small groups presented by Steve Goss and two medical doctors for a comprehensive understanding of that.)The point we wish to make is that neither animism nor Western rationalism is based on how the world actually is. The Bible, however, explains reality to us very clearly. There is an unseen spiritual world that is just as real as the world we can see, touch, and measure. And we need to understand how it works and exercise the authority we have in Christ if we want to avoid becoming a casualty in the spiritual battle that we are in, whether we like it or not.

Understanding the reality of the spiritual world and how it works is vital when it comes to dealing with persistent sin in our lives. Those from a Western worldview background need to be constantly reminded that Satan and demons are real but that, in Christ, it's relatively straightforward to deal with them. And those from an animistic background, whose tendency is to ascribe far too much power to Satan and evil spirits, need to be constantly reminded of their position in Christ—in Him they are now seated with Christ far above all powers and authorities (Ephesians 1:21–22, 2:6), and can exercise that authority very easily and undramatically (James 4:7).

This is an appropriate moment to explain a little more about *The Steps To Experiencing God's Grace*, the ministry component of the course, which is where participants are invited to ask the Holy Spirit to show them areas in their lives where they need to submit to God and adjust their beliefs. We do this during Part C, and there is also a page in the *Participant's Guide* at the end of the notes for this session.

SMALL GROUP TIMINGS

The following plan is designed to help those leading the course in small groups. It assumes a meeting of around ninety minutes in length, and suggests how long each part of the session should last, with an indication of cumulative elapsed time. You will find a time plan in each session. The second column shows the time allocated to each individual element in minutes and seconds. The third column shows the total elapsed time in hours and minutes.

Session 4	Minutes:Seconds	Hours:Minutes
Welcome, Focus, Connect	15:00	00:15
Word Part A	11:00	00:26
Pause For Thought 1	13:00	00:39
Word Part B	12:00	00:51
Pause For Thought 2	13:00	01:04
Word Part C	12:30	01:16
Reflect	13:30	01:30

The time allocated for the Word sections is based on the length of the corresponding section of the videos. Registered users of the course can download an Excel spreadsheet with these timings. Simply enter your own start time, adjust the length of the various components if desired and you will have a customized plan for your session.

For one who has died has been set free from sin.

Romans 6:7

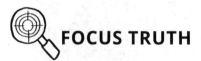

FOCUS TRUTH

No matter what we have done (even as Christians) and no matter how guilty we may feel, the truth is that our guilt has been completely and utterly paid for by Christ's death on the cross so that we can stand confidently before God, who is pure and holy.

CONNECT

Would you rather be a caterpillar or a butterfly? Why?

In Romans 8, Paul speaks to Christians who are facing tough things: he mentions trouble, hardship, persecution, famine, and the ever-present possibility of death. Then he says (verse 37): "In all these things we are more than conquerors through him who loved us."

How have you experienced knowing that you are "more than a conqueror" in Christ in the midst of difficult circumstances?

You might also like to read what Paul says next:

For I am convinced that neither death nor life, neither angels nor demons, neither the present nor the future, nor any powers, neither height nor depth, nor anything else in all creation, will be able to separate us from the love of God that is in Christ Jesus our Lord. (Romans 8:38–39 NIV).

If you watched *The Wonder Of Grace* introductory video for this session, what was the main thing that struck you?

Was there anything in the YouVersion "Daily Nuggets Of Grace" that especially made you think?

PRAYER & DECLARATION

In every session, we want to encourage people to pray out loud and to make a declaration out loud together. A prayer is addressed to God while a declaration is spoken out to the spiritual world in general.

Encourage people to make their declaration boldly!

Heavenly Father,

Thank You that I do not have a high priest who is unable to sympathize with my weaknesses, but one who in every respect has been tempted as I am, yet without sin. I choose to draw near to the throne of grace with confidence, to receive mercy and find grace to help in my time of need. Amen. (see Hebrews 4:15–16)

I DECLARE THAT I AM IDENTIFIED WITH CHRIST NOT ONLY IN HIS DEATH, BUT IN HIS RESURRECTION AND ASCENSION. I AM NOW SEATED WITH HIM AT THE RIGHT HAND OF THE FATHER, THE PLACE OF ULTIMATE POWER AND AUTHORITY, FAR ABOVE EVERY EVIL POWER. I SUBMIT TO GOD AND RESIST THE DEVIL AND DECLARE THAT HE HAS NO CHOICE BUT TO FLEE FROM ME NOW!

WORD

PART A

WHAT YOU *DO* COMES FROM WHO YOU *ARE*

Welcome to "Victorious!," Session 4 of *The Grace Course*!

Did it come as a surprise to understand last time that God doesn't want you to keep feeling guilty after you've gone wrong? Or that He always uses grace rather than guilt to motivate us to do the right thing? Grace just keeps surprising us!

Paul says that we are more than conquerors (Romans 8:37); we are victorious. But maybe it doesn't feel like that to you. In this session, we're going to think about the grace God gives us when we face temptation or when we feel caught in a sin and just don't seem to be able to escape. We've all experienced that, even the apostle Paul—in Romans 7, he says how miserable it made him feel. But he also says that there is a way out.

We'll focus on a key principle: what you *do* comes from who you *are*.

So let's quickly recap what we've said so far about who we now are.

We've seen that the word *sinner* is the usual term in the New Testament for people who don't yet know Jesus, who are spiritually dead. We all *used to be* sinners.

But a great exchange has taken place. Jesus actually *became* sin for us, and we *became* the righteousness of God. And that's why the term the New Testament generally uses for those who know Jesus is *holy ones*. You really are a holy one. Is that sinking in?

2 Corinthians 5:17 is another dramatic statement about who we now are:

Therefore, if anyone is in Christ, he is a new creation. The old has passed away; behold, the new has come.

When we chose to follow Jesus, we became someone totally new. We're as different from how we were before as a butterfly is to a caterpillar—we are totally transformed. Deep down inside our nature is now clean, holy, *nice*.

FREE FROM THE POWER OF SIN

In Romans 6, Paul begins to explain the implications of our new identity for our relationship with sin. We'll join him in verse 7 where he makes this unambiguous statement:

> For one who has died has been set free from sin.

We talked about how most of us have been taught to identify with Jesus in His death on Good Friday. His death dealt with the *penalty* of sin, and we received forgiveness for our sins because of His sacrifice. But Paul is not talking here about *forgiveness* for sin. He's talking about something equally exciting: being set free from *slavery* to sin, from the compulsion to sin.

He continues (verse 8):

> Now if we have died with Christ, we believe that we will also live with him.

As we saw in Session 1, Easter Sunday is not just about celebrating that Jesus conquered death and rose from the dead. The whole point is that *we* have been raised to new life with Christ! And this is the key truth we need to know in order to deal with the *power* of sin. Paul continues (verses 9–10):

> We know that Christ, being raised from the dead, will never die again; death no longer has dominion over him. For the death he died he died to sin, once for all, but the life he lives he lives to God.

When someone you know dies, your relationship with them ends. Now sin hasn't died—in fact it's very much still alive. But Paul says *we* have died with Christ. And our death ended our relationship with sin. Paul's argument is that, just as Christ will never be subject to death again, because we have risen with Him, we need never be subject to slavery to sin again. That is perhaps another surprising fact.

Let's go back and read verse 7 again: "For one who has died has been set free from sin."

Have *you* died with Christ? Yes!

Have you been set free from sin?

Well, if you said yes to the first question, you must say yes to the second one, too! By definition.

But you may very well be thinking, "Well actually, I don't *feel* free from sin. And sometimes I actually do sin."

Paul is well aware of this, so he now gives us three clear instructions based on these great truths. Here's the first (verse 11):

> So you also must consider yourselves dead to sin and alive to God in Christ Jesus.

What does that actually mean in practice?

If you still see yourself as a sinner, albeit a forgiven sinner, what will you do? Sin! What you do comes from who you are, or who you think you are.

But we are much more than just forgiven. We are alive again! We are new creations! We are the righteousness of God! We are holy ones!

[Note: you could insert your own story about struggling with sin or use the following.]

A famous Christian writer, Watchman Nee, struggled for nine years to work out how to "consider himself" dead to sin so that he didn't keep returning to sin. He thought it was like some mind-over-matter thing—like he had to keep "considering" it to be true even though it wasn't, as if that would make it true. But that just didn't work. He was still caught in sin. And he got to the point where he was ready to give up his ministry if he couldn't sort this issue out. One day, he had a light bulb moment and suddenly understood that all he had to do was believe what was actually *already* true. That he was dead to sin and alive to God. And that was it. Suddenly he knew the truth.

And the truth set him free, and he was able to make good choices. From that point on he would go around saying, "Praise the Lord that I am dead!" Perhaps even better would be, "Praise the Lord that I am alive!"

That's great! But if I'm perfectly honest, very often I wake up in the morning and feel very alive to sin and dead to God. And I'm sure the apostle Paul did, too. His encouragement to us is to ignore our feelings and stick to the facts. Whatever we *feel*, the truth is that we *are* now alive to Christ and dead to sin. This is not something we need to strive to *make* true. It just *is* true. We simply need to make a choice to agree with God's Word and live accordingly.

So, is Paul really saying that we don't have to sin? Yes! Because you are a holy one who is risen with Christ to new life, at any given moment you are now genuinely free to make the right choice. What you *do* comes from who you *are*.

PAUSE FOR THOUGHT 1

OBJECTIVE

To understand how knowing our new identity is key to resolving persistent sin in our lives.

1. **In John 8:31–32 Jesus says, "If you hold to my teaching . . . you will know the truth, and the truth will set you free." He goes on to make clear that the freedom He is talking about is freedom from sin: "Very truly I tell you, everyone who sins is a slave to sin. Now a slave has no permanent place in the family, but a son belongs to it forever. So if the Son sets you free, you will be free indeed" (John 8:34–36). How does knowing the truth set us free from slavery to sin? What specific truth do we need to know?**

2. **How does the principle, "What you do comes from who you are," change how you view the possibility of getting free from patterns of persistent sin in your life? What is your key take-away from this principle?**

PART B

THE CONSEQUENCES OF BAD CHOICES

"Wait a minute!" I hear you saying. "If what you *do* comes from who you *are* and I've been a holy one and not a sinner for the last ten years, why have I continued to sin? This principle clearly doesn't work!"

And that's a great question. Let's go back to the image of a butterfly. It was once a creepy, crawly caterpillar, but by the magic of metamorphosis it changed into a totally different creature. And it can fly! You have become a new creation in Christ who can fly above sin. However, if a butterfly gets caught in the rain, it's a sad sight. With wet wings, it ends up crawling slowly along the ground, acting just like a caterpillar.

Even though we're *not* caterpillars any more, we can go back to crawling in sin. We should be flying free like butterflies, but instead we end up *acting* like caterpillars. We're holy ones, but we can *act* like sinners.

When you go wrong, God doesn't come to you and say, "You're a sinner!" His gentle words to us are, in fact, more like this: "Hey, you're my child, you're a holy one, a whole new creation. You're *not* a sinner. So why are you *acting* like one?"

And when you, a holy one, act out of character and sin, it doesn't change God's love for you even a bit. Or the fact that His arms are open for you to return to Him. Or the fact that you are a holy one. But it does affect your fruitfulness.

When we go wrong, we think the problem is that we've disappointed God, that we've let Him down. But Paul's main concern for us is quite different. Let's go back to Romans 6 and Paul's second instruction to us. It's in verse 12:

> Let not sin therefore reign in your mortal body, to make you obey its passions.

Though we have died to sin and ended our relationship with it, sin itself is still very much alive. It's like an "ex."

And it *is* possible for us to rekindle our relationship with our "ex" if we start flirting with sin and hanging out with it. And Paul's concern is this: we can end up hooked again—allowing sin, our nasty "ex," to reign in Jesus' place and to turn us back into its slaves.

SIN IS A SPIRITUAL WARFARE ISSUE

So how do we stop giving sin permission to reign in our bodies? Here's the third instruction (verse 13, emphasis added):

> Do not present your members to sin as instruments for un-righteousness, but present yourselves to God as those who have been brought from death to life, and your members to God as instruments for righteousness.

Think of it this way. If you have a car, you can choose to use it either to give someone in need a ride to church or to deal drugs. In the same way, we have a choice as to how we use our bodies. We can either present ourselves to sin or to God. There's no middle ground. Every day we make that choice.

But here's a crucial factor we might have overlooked. Paul talks about "sin" as if it's a person—have you noticed that?

In Ephesians 4, Paul makes it clear that sin is a spiritual warfare issue. If we let the sun go down on our anger (which is not in itself a sin but just an emotion), we allow it to turn into the sin of unforgiveness, and we give the devil a foothold—a place of influence—in our lives.

We're not living in a world where it's just God and us. It isn't a battle just between us and our flesh. Throughout the Bible, from the garden of Eden in Genesis to the last battle in Revelation, we learn about evil spiritual beings who oppose God and His people. Satan's objective is "to steal and kill and destroy" (John 10:10).

And he will use any foothold you give him through sin to hold you back and obstruct your growth.

OUR WORLDVIEW CAN GET IN THE WAY

The problem is, our worldview can get in the way of understanding this biblically.

If you've grown up in the West, you might acknowledge the existence of the devil and demons theologically, but our worldview predisposes us to ignore the reality of the spiritual world when it comes to living our daily lives. So even though we have the spiritual authority to deal with it, we end up getting duped into doing nothing, and our passivity means the devil keeps a foothold in our lives.

On the other hand, if you've grown up in a different culture, you might have a far greater awareness of the spiritual realm, but the chances are it's one rooted in fear that gives far too much power to the devil and the demonic. And you may think it's more complicated than simply submitting to God and resisting the devil. But it isn't.

AN ANALOGY

Maybe until now you've thought that when we sin, the issue is resolved by saying sorry to God and turning away from the sin, determining to do better. An analogy may help us understand why that isn't enough.

Suppose I was told under no circumstances must I open the door in front of me. But then I hear a voice from behind the door say, "Help! Let me out, I'm trapped!" So, I open the door when no one is looking. And out comes a huge dog which sinks its teeth into my leg and won't let go. The voice now turns mean. "That was stupid! What were you thinking, you failure?"

The problem is, this dog is invisible. All I know is I did something wrong, and now I'm in pain and feel terrible. Who do I get angry with—the dog? No, because I don't know it's there. I get angry with myself.

I confess: "Father God, I opened the door. Please forgive me!" Does He? Of course. In fact, I'm already forgiven.

But I'm still walking around, limping, with an invisible dog hanging off my leg telling me I'm a failure! And that will short-circuit God's power to enable me to live righteously. It makes it difficult for me to resist further temptation or make the right choice.

And the more I seem unable to get out of the cycle, the more the enemy accuses me and the more shame I feel for what I've done.

If we open the door, we allow sin to reign, to become our master. Just confessing sin isn't enough. Remember, James 4:7 gives us two things to do: submit *and* resist.

Confession is part of submitting. But we mustn't stop there. We finish the job by actively resisting the devil and reclaiming the place of influence that our sin gave him.

Back to our analogy: I start by confessing "Father God, I opened the door. Please forgive me." Then I tell the dog to let go of my leg and be gone. But why would the dog obey me? Because of who I am now. All of us are identified with Christ, not only in His death and His resurrection, but also in His ascension to the right hand of the Father, where we are seated with Him right now far above all other powers including Satan (Ephesians 2:6).

Coming back to Paul writing to the Romans, he finishes with an amazingly encouraging statement, for anyone who feels stuck (verse 14):

> For sin will have no dominion over you, since you are not under law but under grace.

SUMMARY

Even when we go wrong, we are still under God's grace—not some legalistic system that demands a punishment. And if we have allowed sin to reign, we can resolve it. We've talked about three things:

Submit to God *and* resist the devil;

Know that you are now dead to sin and alive to God;

Make the choice every day not to let sin reign in your body by offering every part of your body to God rather than to sin.

In any area of your life you are either free or you are a slave. You don't *grow* into freedom. You *take hold* of it.

PAUSE FOR THOUGHT 2

OBJECTIVE

To understand that temptation and sin are spiritual warfare issues.

1. **In what ways does the worldview you grew up with either minimize or exaggerate the reality and power of "the spiritual forces of evil in the heavenly realms" (Ephesians 6:12)?**

2. **"In any area of your life you are either free or you are a slave. You don't grow into freedom. You take hold of it." How might this principle change the way you approach getting out of patterns of persistent sin?**

PART C

TAKE THE WAY OUT OF TEMPTATION

In Session 2, I shared how I just couldn't seem to get victory over pornography. What I didn't realize at the time was that the temptation was so intense because I had opened the door to that invisible dog. It wasn't just a question of will power. I was in a spiritual battle.

Years later, when I learned how to deal with the reality of evil spirits around me, I submitted to God and took authority in Christ and commanded them to leave . . . and I immediately knew something changed within me. Not long after that, I was alone in a hotel and the TV came on by itself, as if the powers of evil were luring me to view things that were not pure. Overcoming the temptation that time was immediate. All I had to do was turn off the TV and go on with my day.

The Steps To Freedom In Christ and *The Steps To Experiencing God's Grace* are great ways to submit to God and resist the devil. We ask the Holy Spirit to show us where there are footholds of the enemy in our lives. We then renounce them and repent of them. To renounce something is to declare to God, and to the unseen spiritual world, that our agreement with, allegiance to, and our participation in that thing is over. To repent means to change our mind about our sin and turn away from it.

There's more about *The Steps* in your notes for this session. For many people it's an absolutely life-changing process during which we begin to understand the deception we've suffered from. Then we can go on to renew our minds so that we really *know* the truth deep in our hearts.

So how can we resist temptation? The first thing, then, is to ensure we've closed all the doors we opened to the enemy.

Then we have a very specific promise from God in 1 Corinthians 10:13 (NIV): "No temptation has overtaken you except what is common to mankind. And God is faithful; he will not let you be tempted beyond what you can bear. But when you are tempted, he will also provide a way out so that you can endure it."

I used to get really irritated with that verse because it didn't seem that there was a way out. The temptation was just so intense. Where is the way of escape? But I now know that this way of escape, the "fire exit" if you like, is always right at the beginning of the process of being tempted. You have to recognize the exit and take it immediately.

Let's say I'm single and I meet my boyfriend at a restaurant. After dinner, it's late but "we're in the middle of a great conversation." So I propose going to my apartment "to continue talking." In my apartment, I pull out some wine and we draw closer as we talk. One thing leads to another, and we end up crossing boundaries we did *not* intend to cross.

I can rationalize as much as I like, but let's be real. As soon as I proposed going to my apartment, the desire to give in to my passions was there—even if I didn't admit it to myself.

Where was the fire exit? Right at the beginning, when the apparently innocent thought about continuing to talk first came to mind. That was my chance to "take captive every thought to make it obedient to Christ" (2 Corinthians 10:5 NIV). We need to learn to *recognize* that innocent-seeming thought for what it actually is—temptation—and throw it out as soon as it appears.

Regarding sexual temptation, "Don't think you can be holier than David, wiser than Solomon, or stronger than Samson."

Every temptation is an attempt to persuade you to live your life independently of God. Satan knows your history and exactly where you're vulnerable, and that's where he will attack. His aim is to persuade you to try to meet your entirely legitimate needs for acceptance, significance, and security using something other than God.

But God has promised to "meet all your needs according to his glorious riches in Christ Jesus" (Philippians 4:19 NIV), and we need to learn to find satisfaction only in Him.

That means that every temptation is based on a lie. Does money really give you permanent security? No! Can another person really fulfill your need to be accepted? Not completely. Does getting people to like you really make you significant? Of course not.

What are the temptations you face most often? Can you figure out what lies the enemy is feeding you to persuade you to fall for them? You can be sure that it will be accompanied by another huge lie—the one that says that your specific sin is "no big deal."

I have been a slave to the language of the kingdom of darkness: complaint and criticism. I was very fluent and practiced it often with my husband, my kids, and even God. I cried bitterly when the Holy Spirit showed me how much harm my words caused and how blind I had been. So I submitted to God and resisted the devil, to close the "door" I had opened to the enemy. Then the Lord addressed the heart issue: a deep dissatisfaction. My baggage of unmet emotional needs plus ministry hardships had fed the lie that I was empty, needy, hungry. Jesus said, "My grace is sufficient for you," and His grace flooded and filled my void. Now I present my tongue daily to God as an instrument to do good, and I'm learning the language of the kingdom of Heaven: praise and thanksgiving. I'm far from fluent, but I'm learning.

Father God wants His people to obey Him, not because they *have* to but because they *choose* to, out of love and respect. Freedom puts you in the position where you *can* choose, free from spiritual entanglement.

DRAW NEAR TO THE THRONE OF GRACE

As we finish this session, we want you to hear some powerful, refreshing words of grace about Jesus, who is our great High Priest:

"For we do not have a high priest who is unable to sympathize with our weaknesses, but one who in every respect has been tempted as we are, yet without sin" (Hebrews 4:15).

He totally gets it. He understands! He knows what it's like to live in this fallen world with temptation on every side. He didn't fall for it Himself, but He knows your weaknesses. And He doesn't condemn you for them. He actually sympathizes with you.

> Let us then with confidence draw near to the throne of grace, that we may receive mercy and find grace to help in time of need. (Hebrews 4:15–16)

His heart is always that we should draw near with confidence, not crawl in like miserable worms. If we've gone wrong, we'll find nothing but mercy, forgiveness and understanding. If we're facing temptation, we'll find grace to overcome.

God loves you so much. No matter where you are right now, He has things for you to do, and fruit for you to bear.

What you *do* comes from who you *are*. And you are a pure, holy child of the Living God. You are victorious. In fact you are *more* than a conqueror in Christ!

Draw near. Receive mercy. Find grace to help in your time of need.

REFLECT

Introduction

We've said that behind every temptation is a lie, usually along the lines that you can get your needs for significance, security, and acceptance met through something other than your relationship with God.

Reflection

Ask the Holy Spirit to speak to you about the two or three temptations that you are most vulnerable to. Write them down. Ask Him why you are particularly vulnerable to these things—is it because of past experiences, for example?

For each one, ask God to identify the lie your vulnerability to sin is based on. Can you think of Bible verses you could use to counteract the lies?

> CONCLUDING THE SESSION

Participants will get a chance to address sin-confess cycles in *The Steps To Experiencing God's Grace* but some might want to make a start today. Point out the "Breaking Sin-Confess Cycles" exercise in the Participant's Guide and below.

Remind participants about "Daily Nuggets Of Grace," the devotional that accompanies this course that can be accessed on the YouVersion Bible App, *The Wonder Of Grace* introductory videos, and *The Grace Connection*, the book that accompanies *The Grace Course*.

If you have a date for an Away Day to go through *The Steps To Experiencing God's Grace*, ensure that participants have it in their calendars.

Close in prayer.

> BREAKING SIN-CONFESS CYCLES

[This is a powerful exercise for people who are caught in a sin. Make sure that you draw people's attention to it at the end of the session. It is also in the Participant's Guide.]

Are you frustrated by returning again and again to the same sins?

We invite you to speak out loud the following declaration (based on Romans 6 and James 4).

Instead of depending on your own strength and making rules for yourself to try to keep from sinning, you can enjoy living in the reality of your new identity, Christ in you the hope of glory (Colossians 1:27). Speak it out every day as long as it takes.

I DECLARE THAT I AM NOW A NEW CREATION IN CHRIST. I AM DEAD TO SIN AND ALIVE TO GOD. I CONFESS MY SINS [SPECIFICALLY NAME ANY HABITUAL SINS] AND TURN AWAY FROM THEM.

I SPECIFICALLY DECLARE THAT THE SIN OF [SPECIFICALLY NAME ANY HABITUAL SINS ONE BY ONE] DOES NOT RULE ME ANY LONGER AND I RENOUNCE ITS CONTROL OF ME. JESUS, WHO LIVES IN ME, IS MY LOVING MASTER AND RULER AND ALL THAT I AM NOW BELONGS TO HIM.

Thank You, Jesus, that You have made me a saint, a holy one, so I CAN glorify You in my body. Therefore, I refuse to offer my body to be used to commit unrighteousness. Instead, I submit all that I am to my Heavenly Father who raised me to life with Christ. I now gladly offer the parts of my body: my heart, eyes, ears, mouth, tongue, hands, feet, sexual organs, mind, understanding, mental powers, emotions, imagination, and reasoning to God, and I choose to use these parts of my body only for righteousness, completely relying on the power of His Holy Spirit within me to accomplish this.

So I submit myself completely to God and resist the devil who must flee from me now (James 4:7).

FREEDOM IN CHRIST

session **05**

COURAGEOUS!

OBJECTIVE

To understand how to deal with unhealthy fears so that they do not control us.

LEADER'S NOTES

Most people are not aware that they are a slave to unhealthy fears because they have simply learned to live with them, but we hope that this session will help them realize their presence and take the necessary steps to deal with them. As our Focus Verse makes clear, understanding God's gracious love is the starting point for resolving fear.

We do not want to teach people just the theory. We want them to experience how they can practically resolve unhealthy fears through grace.

In the videos, our presenters share a lot of personal examples of fearful occurrences in their lives and how they learned to overcome them. Before you lead the session, you might like to consider some stories that you could share personally or perhaps prepare another member of the group to share. There is nothing like real testimony to encourage people that they, too, can resolve issues that might otherwise appear to be impossible to resolve.

SMALL GROUP TIMINGS

The following plan is designed to help those leading the course in small groups. It assumes a meeting of around ninety minutes in length, and suggests how long each part of the session should last, with an indication of cumulative elapsed time. You will find a time plan in each session. The second column shows the time allocated to each individual element in minutes and seconds. The third column shows the total elapsed time in hours and minutes.

Session 5	Minutes:Seconds	Hours:Minutes
Welcome, Focus, Connect	15:00	00:15
Word Part A	12:00	00:27
Pause For Thought 1	12:00	00:39
Word Part B	12:00	00:51
Pause For Thought 2	15:00	01:06
Word Part C	11:00	01:17
Reflect	13:00	01:30

The time allocated for the Word sections is based on the length of the corresponding section of the videos. Registered users of the course can download an Excel spreadsheet with these timings. Simply enter your own start time, adjust the length of the various components if desired and you will have a customized plan for your session.

FOCUS VERSE

There is no fear in love, but perfect love casts out fear. For fear has to do with punishment, and whoever fears has not been perfected in love.

1 John 4:18

FOCUS TRUTH

We do not have to allow unhealthy fears to control us or set the agenda in our lives because God is all-powerful and everywhere-present and has given us grace gifts of power, love, and sound judgment.

CONNECT

What were some of the things you were afraid of when growing up?

Read Isaiah 41:10 (NIV) out loud together:

> So do not fear, for I am with you; do not be dismayed, for I am your God. I will strengthen you and help you; I will uphold you with my righteous right hand.

Thank God for these truths.

If you watched *The Wonder Of Grace* introductory video for this session, what was the main thing that struck you?

Was there anything in the YouVersion "Daily Nuggets Of Grace" that especially made you think?

PRAYER & DECLARATION

In every session, we want to encourage people to pray out loud and to make a declaration out loud together. A prayer is addressed to God while a declaration is spoken out to the spiritual world in general.

Encourage people to make their declaration boldly!

Dear Heavenly Father, thank You that You have promised that You will not leave me or forsake me, and You tell me to be strong and courageous (Joshua 1:5–6). Thank You that Your grace and love are far stronger than any of my fears, so I can confidently say, You are my helper, I will not fear (Hebrews 13:5–6). I will continually praise You and worship You so that I dwell in the truth that You, the all-knowing, everywhere-present, all-powerful, and absolutely loving God of grace, are with me and in me! Amen.

I DECLARE THE TRUTH THAT GOD HAS NOT GIVEN ME A SPIRIT OF FEAR, BUT OF POWER AND LOVE AND A SOUND MIND (2 TIMOTHY 1:7). JESUS IS MY LORD AND I TELL EVERY ENEMY OF CHRIST TO LEAVE ME NOW. THE SPIRIT I RECEIVED DOES NOT MAKE ME A SLAVE SO THAT I LIVE IN FEAR AGAIN; RATHER, THE SPIRIT I RECEIVED BROUGHT ABOUT MY ADOPTION TO SONSHIP. AND BY HIM I CRY, "ABBA, FATHER" (ROMANS 8:15). GOD IS ON MY SIDE AND WILL DELIVER ME FROM ALL MY FEARS. I AM A BELOVED CHILD OF GOD AND THERE IS NOW NO CONDEMNATION FOR ME BECAUSE I AM IN CHRIST JESUS (ROMANS 8:1).

WORD

PART A

COURAGE IS NOT THE ABSENCE OF FEAR

Welcome to "Courageous!," the fifth session of *The Grace Course*!

We saw last time that what we *do* should spring naturally from who we *are*. Ephesians 2:10 (NIV, emphasis added) expresses that wonderfully. It says, "For we *are* God's handiwork, created in Christ Jesus to do good works, which God prepared in advance for us to do." *Handiwork* literally means "a work of art"—you were *not* mass produced; you were *crafted*.

And because of who you now are, God has prepared some specific things for you to do. He doesn't *need* your help, of course, but in His grace, He invites you to work with Him.

Maybe that thought fills you with excitement. But it can also be quite scary.

While working with a ministry in Uganda, we had a vision to build a Prayer Mountain, and God blessed us with the money we needed to purchase the land. But very quickly things started to go very wrong. We were subject to an organized land grab—one night a gang came, planted tree seedlings everywhere, erected a fence, and the next thing we knew we were summoned to court accused of trespassing on their land! These people were clearly violent criminals, blatantly attempting to steal our land, but their claims were taken seriously by the authorities. At one point we were facing five civil suits and four criminal cases of trespass—on our own

land! Two of my fellow elders were fraudulently arrested. I had to go to court day after day for months, all the time experiencing intimidation from this gang who regularly resorted to violence and threats to kill us. It was horrible. I don't think I've ever felt so afraid or prayed so much! Even thinking about it ten years later makes me break out in a cold sweat. I found myself thinking a fair bit about Joshua.

After decades of wandering around the wilderness, the Israelites were to cross the river Jordan and take the land that had been promised to them. And God wanted Joshua to lead them.

That would have been fine if the land was empty. But it wasn't. It was full of people who were exceptionally large and scary. They had a nasty array of weapons, and they were definitely not going to welcome him with open arms!

We get an idea about how Joshua was feeling by what God says to him:

> "Just as I was with Moses, so I will be with you. I will not leave you or forsake you. Be strong and courageous." (Joshua 1:5–6)

God then repeats Himself twice: "Only be strong and very courageous" (verse 7) because Joshua was clearly feeling quite the opposite—weak and frightened.

And He adds an instruction, "being careful to do according to all the law that Moses my servant commanded you . . . that you may have good success wherever you go" (verse 7).

There was just one thing Joshua was told to do, and that was to carefully follow God's instructions, God's law. If he did that, God promised him success in this crazy venture to take the land with a ragtag bunch of wilderness wanderers.

During that land grab, I experienced real, gut-wrenching fear every single day—I mean, people really were coming after us with machetes.

But courage is not the absence of fear. It's making the right choice in the face of that fear.

We knew what God had put in front of us and that He was bigger than the mob. We pressed on through that daily intimidation.

But I had to cling on to God's Word. In those dark moments when I was most afraid, I would declare out loud "You keep in perfect peace those who trust in you"—that's from Isaiah 26—and, from Ephesians, "I am a holy one. I am seated with Christ in the heavenly realms. I submit myself to God and I command Satan and every evil spirit to leave my presence now."

It was the only thing that made a real, tangible difference. And it was the only way I got through it.

Today there's a church on the land, and praise, worship and prayer retreats happen regularly. It would have been so easy to let fear dictate our actions. But that would have led to a very different outcome.

Fear is another false motivator. We'll see in today's session that, counterintuitively, it's grace that enables us to walk free of it.

WHAT IS FEAR?

What is fear? It's an emotional reaction to a perception of impending danger or harm that triggers a physical response in our bodies.

When we're confronted by a dangerous situation, our brain quickly evaluates whether it's better to stay and fight, to run away, to keep very still, or to appease the threat. It then sends a signal to our adrenal glands, which pump hormones through our bodies so that we can react rapidly. Now that's a good thing. We need to have a healthy fear of things that could harm us.

Healthy fear is fear that makes sense. You don't try and pet a snarling, frothing-at-the-mouth dog. Or large, venomous spiders. Stuff like that.

But then there's also **unhealthy fear**. That's fear that is an unreasonable or disproportionate response to what is happening. For example, being afraid of *all* spiders, even the tiny ones that can't harm you at all.

An unhealthy fear works like a boa constrictor. Unlike snakes that kill by injecting venom, boas kill you with a tight hug. This long and heavy snake bites for an anchor and then coils itself around the victim. Each time the victim breathes out, the coils tighten and tighten until the victim is unable to breathe.

Unhealthy fears gradually squeeze the joy out of living, making our world smaller and smaller. An example might be someone who is afraid of heights may take an alternative route to work to avoid crossing a bridge. Or maybe end up making bigger life decisions—like taking a new job closer to home when a better one was offered farther away, but it was the other side of the bridge.

More severe fears are known as **phobias;** sometimes they can become so suffocating you experience agoraphobia (literally "fear of the marketplace") and don't want to go out at all.

We may not all have phobias but most of us are vulnerable to unhealthy fears that can limit what we do if we don't address them.Maybe we fear talking to people about Jesus., so we simply don't do it and have no expectation of doing it, ever.

Maybe we fear not having enough money, so we hold on tightly to what we have and end up working three jobs to the detriment of our family or a stressful, all-consuming job to the detriment of our health.

Many of us have a fear of failure that tempts us not to take risks, like asking a person out for coffee or discipling a young believer.

Fear immobilizes us. It confuses us. It makes it difficult to think straight.

At the height of the opposition we experienced in Uganda, I got paranoid. I started thinking that every loudspeaker announcement, every local resident, every local radio phone-in was stirring others up against us. Whenever my phone rang, it would send me into a panic.

We lose perspective, and it overwhelms us. All you can think about is yourself—your own safety, your own protection, or your own reputation.

LOVE CASTS OUT FEAR

When fear grips us, we need to come back to the truth of God's Word. The writer to the Hebrews says, "He has said, 'I will never leave you nor forsake you.' So we can confidently say, 'The Lord is my helper; I will not fear'" (Hebrews 13:5–6).

And John says, "There is no fear in love; but perfect love casts out fear" (1 John 4:18).

No matter how it *feels*, that's the truth—we can either live in God's grace or in fear. The great news is that His love is far stronger than any of our fears.

PAUSE FOR THOUGHT 1

OBJECTIVE

To come to grips with the difference between healthy and unhealthy fears.

1. **What unhealthy fears have you seen at work in your life or in the lives of others? How do you know that they were unhealthy rather than legitimate fears?**

2. **"There is no fear in love; but perfect love casts out fear" (1 John 4:18). How do you think this might work in practice?**

PART B

OVERCOMING UNHEALTHY FEARS

There are three grace gifts that enable us to deal a death blow to unhealthy fears. 2 Timothy 1:7 (CSB, emphasis added) tells us about them: "For God has not given us a spirit of fear, but of *power*, *love,* and *sound judgment*."

So how do we get them? Well, the verb tense in this verse is past tense. We already have them! We just need to learn how to use them.

POWER

The first gift God has bestowed on us by His grace is the gift of power. Let me pray for you using some amazing words that Paul prayed for the Ephesians: "I pray that the eyes of your heart may be enlightened in order that you may know the hope to which he has called you, the riches of his glorious inheritance in his holy people, and his incomparably great *power* for us who believe" (Ephesians 1:18–19 NIV, emphasis added). Amen!

Paul doesn't pray that you will *receive* that power; he's praying that you will *know* the power you already have. That's a subtle but very important point. He goes on to say, "That power is the same as the mighty strength he exerted when he raised Christ from the dead and seated him at his right hand in the heavenly realms, far above all rule and authority, power and dominion, and every name that is invoked, not only in the present age but also in the one to come" (Ephesians 1:19–21 NIV).

Think about the power that raised Christ from the dead. Now that's power! And he's talking about spiritual power. Which is why he mentions Christ's position in the heavenly realms far above all other powers and authorities, meaning demonic powers.

And you already have it—simply because you are in Christ.

About eight years ago I was asked to teach God's Word regularly inside a local prison. The first time I entered that prison alone, I was pretty much terrified. Through the big inner gates leading to the prison courtyard, I could see nearly two hundred inmates waiting to hear what I had to say. As I

stepped through the gate and heard it being locked behind me, I turned to talk to the officer only to discover that he was still on the back side of the gate. I wanted to run away!

The thought in my mind was, "You have nothing to tell these people. What do you even have in common with them?"

When you realize what's going on, that this thought is from the enemy, you can use the power God gives. You can say, "Jesus is my Lord, and I tell every enemy of Christ to leave now." You can declare a truth from God's Word: "I declare that the Holy Spirit will give me the right words" because that's what Jesus promised (see Luke 12:12).

That first day in the prison was the start of more than I ever imagined. We've seen men and women come to Christ. Inmates' lives have been changed by learning God's truth. They've testified to judges, to family members, and to new inmates of the way Jesus' love has changed their lives. And God has grown the ministry to the point that our team now teaches regularly in ten prisons.

LOVE

The second gift that you already have, by God's grace, is **love.** Let's look again at what John had to say about this gift of love:

"There is no fear in love; but perfect love casts out fear, because fear involves punishment, and the one who fears is not perfected in love." (1 John 4:18 lsb)

If you still believe that God is going to punish you, or is disappointed with you, or that He will stop loving you, then it's impossible to trust Him fully. As a result, you're thrown back onto your own efforts to try to deal with your fears. And that's a scary, lonely place to be.

But if you remember who you are, a beloved child of God, and that "there is therefore now no condemnation for those who are in Christ Jesus" (Romans 8:1), the fear of His punishment is destroyed.

Again, this is about going to God's Word and reminding ourselves about God's true nature. And about our new identity as holy ones.

SOUND JUDGMENT

Which brings us to the third gift of God's grace, sound judgment, sometimes translated as "a sound mind."

Fear distorts the truth. In fact, every unhealthy fear is based on a lie. So exercising sound judgment simply boils down—again!—to coming back to God's Word and making a choice to see things the way God sees them; in other words, how they really are.

God told Joshua not to turn from His Law to the right or the left so that he would have success wherever he went. It's the same for us. Making your life count as a disciple of Jesus comes from relentlessly choosing to live according to what God, in His love, tells you in His Word, and to trust God more than you trust the scary thoughts in your mind.

How can we apply sound judgment to unhealthy fears?

In Africa, I've had some close encounters with snakes, and when I do, I sweat from every pore in my body. Is that a healthy fear?

Well, let me give you two scenarios.

One time, I bent over to pick up a ball in the yard when I suddenly saw a cobra laying there, its mouth open, fangs out. Healthy fear? Yes, because that thing could kill me.

Another time, I was playing outside with my young kids while we were visiting North America. At the edge of the yard, I saw a snake coiled around a pole. I yelled for the kids to stay away, and ran and got a big stick. As I cautiously approached the snake, it never moved. I came to discover it was a toy snake, made of rubber, that someone had wrapped around the pole. Healthy fear? No, because it could not harm me.

For us to have a legitimate healthy fear of something, the thing that we're afraid of must have two qualities. It must be 1) present *and* 2) powerful.

The cobra was both present and powerful—healthy fear. But a rubber snake? Although present, it had absolutely *no power*—so no need to be afraid.

Here's the point: every unhealthy fear comes from believing that the thing we're afraid of is both present *and* powerful when in fact it isn't.

Let's apply this principle to the two greatest fears people tend to have, the fear of death and the fear of other people.

THE FEAR OF DEATH

Can you remove the *presence* of death? No, unless Jesus comes back first, every one of us is going to experience physical death, and none of us knows when death will show up. But what about its *power*?

Hebrews 2:14–15 says that Christ died, *"that through death He might render powerless him who had the power of death, that is, the devil, and might free those who through fear of death were subject to slavery all their lives"* (LSB, emphasis added).

And Paul says graphically that death has lost its sting (see 1 Corinthians 15:55). *Even when you're facing people with machetes.*

But even though the devil is powerless, he can *deceive* us into continuing to live in the fear of death and being slaves to that fear all our lives by making us believe that death is still powerful.

In order for us to be free from slavery to the fear of death, we need to *know* the truth that sets us free. Which is, *"For to me, to live is Christ, and to die is gain"* (Philippians 1:21). If you belong to Jesus, when you die physically, it just gets better. Physical death actually opens the door for you to be with Him in a very tangible way and to experience all the joys of heaven. Death has no power over us whatsoever!

PAUSE FOR THOUGHT 2

OBJECTIVE

To understand the concept that there is a lie behind every unhealthy fear and to start to uncover some of those lies and the corresponding Biblical truth.

1. "Behind every unhealthy fear is a lie." Look at the fears below. If someone is prone to those fears, what lies might they believe? For example, a possible lie for [1] is "Satan is more powerful than I am."

   • Fear of Satan and powers of darkness

   • Fear of the future

   • Fear of rejection

   • Fear of failure

   • Fear of confrontation

   • Fear of financial problems

2. What truths from God's Word can you find for each lie? For example, for (1) a good verse would be James 4:7: "Submit... to God. Resist the devil, and he will flee from you."

PART C

THE FEAR OF PEOPLE

Let's turn now to the fear of other people. Proverbs 29:25 says, "The fear of man lays a snare, but whoever trusts in the LORD is safe."

Let's say you've got a huge fear of your boss. He's an intimidating person perhaps, but right now you are not afraid of him are you? Why not? He's not here. But when you go to work on Monday morning, there he is.

When you are at the coffee machine, having a cup of coffee with your colleagues, you are not afraid of him then are you? Because he's over on the other side of the building in his office. Powerful but not present. In fact, you may well want to get off your chest what you think about his character. You are well into your story and completely oblivious. But eventually you turn around and see him—standing there, hands on hips, with a tight smile on his face. Now the fear is healthy! Powerful *and* present.

Or is it? Because we're told not to fear people. So what can you do to stop the boss from exercising that kind of fear over you even when he's present? You have to get rid of one of those attributes. He's a big guy, so you can't do anything about the fact that he's present. So what about powerful?

Well, exactly what power does he have over you in the worst-case scenario? "He might be able to fire me." True. How can you deal with that? Resign! Well, you don't have to write the letter—but be willing to if you must.

Is this fear powerful? Well that depends. . . . On what? On you! By exercising the sound judgment that God has already given you, by resolving in your own mind today that, if push comes to shove, you will always obey God rather than people and take His opinion of you rather than theirs, you have in effect removed their power. They may be present, but they are no longer powerful.

We need to come to the point where we resolve that our allegiance to King Jesus comes before anything else. Even if those closest to us disapprove of what we're doing for Him, as long as we know that it's the right thing, we will not be afraid of them or their disapproval or rejection but will choose to do the right thing.

In Psalm 56, David gives us the bottom line. "What can man do to me?" he asks (verse 11). And then he answers his own question: "Nothing." He didn't write this in the comfort of his palace but while he was in the hands of his enemies! He had resolved that he could face the worst-case scenario if he was walking in obedience. Above it all . . . God was in charge. The danger from his enemies was *present*, but in light of the Creator of the universe, it wasn't *powerful*.

LIVING IN FREEDOM FROM FEAR

How do you live in freedom from fear?

1. DEAL WITH SIN ISSUES

First, fear first appeared right after Adam and Eve rebelled. God asked them, "Where are you?" and Adam's response was, "I heard you were in the garden, and I was **afraid** because I was naked; so I hid" (Genesis 3:9–10 NIV, emphasis added).

Sin caused them to feel fear for the first time. And unresolved sin leaves us vulnerable to fear today, too. Because it gives the enemy a position of influence in our lives.

So I make it a habit to go through *The Steps To Freedom In Christ* regularly—I do it at least once a year and sometimes in between when I realize something is a bit off.

2. RECOGNIZE THAT GOD IS ALWAYS PRESENT *AND* ALL POWERFUL

Secondly, recognize that there is just one fear that is always healthy. The fear of God. Why? Because God is always present and all-powerful.

Perhaps "the fear of God" sounds like we're supposed to be afraid of Him. But nothing could be further from the truth. Listen to Romans 8:14–15 (NIV):

"For those who are led by the Spirit of God are the children of God. The Spirit you received does not make you slaves, so that you live in fear again; rather, the Spirit you received brought about your adoption to sonship. And by him we cry, 'Abba, Father.'"

As God's children, the Holy Spirit moves us to cry out "Daddy!"

Fear of the Lord is more like profound awe, a realization of our smallness next to His infinite greatness, a willing submission to our loving Lord and King.

God *is* love. He's on our side! David worked out how to make that truth real. He said, "I sought the LORD, and He answered me, and delivered me from all my fears" (Psalm 34:4 NIV).

"Fear not" is only learned in relationship. Cultivate a lifestyle of praise and worship so that you dwell in the truth that the all-knowing, everywhere-present, all-powerful, and absolutely loving God of grace is with you and in you! What can a person or anything else do to you? Nothing! Absolutely nothing!

3. RENEW YOUR MIND

And thirdly, learn to renew your mind to God's truth. As we've seen, behind every unhealthy fear is a lie. In order to root out the fear, we need to identify the lie.

A few years ago, after five moves across the Atlantic in ten years, the possibility of another one brought fear. Fear that wandering was my destiny, fear of never settling down, fear of not having a place to call home, fear of not developing relational roots anywhere . . . The thought of another move gave me the same sensation in my stomach as looking down a precipice—panic!

I set out to find the lie behind that fear. Some wise friends helped me discover that relationships have the highest value for my temperament; that when I connect with people, I feel accepted; that close, intimate relationships make me feel significant; and that I feel secure when I belong. The lie was that lack of connection made me insignificant, rejected and insecure. You might as well kill me . . .Once you have the lie, you need to replace it with the truth from God's Word. That's what will transform you.

Through His Word God said: "I am yours and you are mine, bury your roots deeply in my love. I will satisfy you. Come, let me be the lover of your soul. Let us, Father, Son and Spirit, be your family and source of community. But you are also a foreigner and a pilgrim. Don't forget it, and await your heavenly homeland. That's where you truly belong."

Before the end of *The Grace Course*, we'll introduce you to Stronghold-Busting, a practical strategy to renew your mind. Imagine how different life would be if you were free from those fears—it's entirely possible!

In the next session, we'll consider fear's sibling, anxiety.

For now, remember:

> "There is no fear in love; but perfect love casts out fear" (1 John 4:18).

REFLECT

Introduction

As we've seen, the one fear that is always healthy is the fear of God because He is always present and all-powerful. Of course we don't need to be afraid of our loving Father. But we do need to develop a healthy awe of just who He is and how powerful He is.

Reflection

Read Psalm 145 slowly. Let the words sink in, perhaps by reading it in different versions. Thank God for who He is and what He does. Remind yourself that God never changes and that He is the one who loves you, who is always with you, and who will never leave you nor forsake you.

> CONCLUDING THE SESSION

Remind participants about "Daily Nuggets Of Grace," the devotional that accompanies this course that can be accessed on the YouVersion Bible App, *The Wonder Of Grace* introductory videos, and *The Grace Connection*, the book that accompanies *The Grace Course*.

If you have a date for an Away Day to go through *The Steps To Experiencing God's Grace*, ensure that participants have it in their calendars.

Close in prayer.

FREEDOM
IN CHRIST

session **06**

CALM!

OBJECTIVE

To equip us with practical Biblical principles that
will enable us to cast our anxiety onto Christ
and live a life free from inappropriate concern.

LEADER'S NOTES

We know that anxiety can have complex causes such as stress or past trauma, but whatever its cause, any Christian who is prone to it will benefit hugely from understanding and putting into practice the Biblical truths outlined in this session.

This session (Part B especially) teaches the specific principles that participants will be invited to put into practice when they go through Step Six of *The Steps To Experiencing God's Grace*, which is called "Exchanging Anxiety For God's Peace."

We hope that they will then go on to use them throughout the rest of their lives, whenever they realize that anxiety has begun to take hold.

In Part C and the Reflect that follows, we read the "My Father God" list of Biblical truths. Many struggle to see God as the God of love and grace that He is because their concept of "father" has been conditioned by their experiences of their earthly fathers. Try to help them understand that God is not like our earthly fathers—He's so much better in every way. No matter how good your earthly father was, he was nowhere near as good as God. Suggest that people declare this list out loud for six weeks or so if they sense that they need to bring their view of God in line with how He actually is. For many people, this has been life-changing.

We have included two additional items at the end of the notes for this session, *Dwelling In Appreciation* and *Physical Tips to Combat Anxiety*. These are optional exercises that participants may find helpful.

SMALL GROUP TIMINGS

The following plan is designed to help those leading the course in small groups. It assumes a meeting of around ninety minutes in length, and suggests how long each part of the session should last, with an indication of cumulative elapsed time. You will find a time plan in each session. The second column shows the time allocated to each individual element in minutes and seconds. The third column shows the total elapsed time in hours and minutes.

Session 6	Minutes:Seconds	Hours:Minutes
Welcome, Focus, Connect	12:00	00:12
Word Part A	11:00	00:23
Pause For Thought 1	14:00	00:37
Word Part B	11:00	00:48
Pause For Thought 2	14:00	01:02
Word Part C	12:00	01:14
Reflect	16:00	01:30

The time allocated for the Word sections is based on the length of the corresponding section of the videos. Registered users of the course can download an Excel spreadsheet with these timings. Simply enter your own start time, adjust the length of the various components if desired and you will have a customized plan for your session.

FOCUS VERSE

Cast all your anxiety on him because he cares for you.

1 Peter 5:7 NIV

FOCUS TRUTH

Knowing the character of your Heavenly Father enables you to cast all your anxiety on Him.

CONNECT

Share a recent picture from your phone or memory that makes you smile.

"I keep my eyes always on the LORD. With him at my right hand, I will not be shaken" (Psalm 16:8 NIV). In times of uncertainty, what character quality of God brings you hope?

If you watched *The Wonder Of Grace* introductory video for this session, what was the main thing that struck you?

Was there anything in the YouVersion "Daily Nuggets Of Grace" that especially made you think?

PRAYER & DECLARATION

In every session, we want to encourage people to pray out loud and to make a declaration out loud together. A prayer is addressed to God while a declaration is spoken out to the spiritual world in general.

Encourage people to make their declaration boldly!

Dear Heavenly Father, Your Word tells us not to be anxious about tomorrow (Matthew 6:34) or indeed about anything at all (Philippians 4:6). Thank You that living in Your grace can prevent us from being at the mercy of every anxious thought, no matter what our circumstances. Please help us to understand how to cast all our anxiety on You, and to know at an even deeper level that You really care for us (1 Peter 5:6–7). We want to know You as You really are. Amen.

I RECOGNIZE THAT SATAN IS ACTIVELY TRYING TO GET ME INTO ANXIETY AND TO EXPLOIT THE DOUBLE-MINDEDNESS IT CAUSES. BUT I CHOOSE THE TRUTH OF GOD'S WORD WHICH TELLS ME TO BE ANXIOUS FOR NOTHING, BUT IN EVERYTHING BY PRAYER AND SUPPLICATION WITH THANKSGIVING TO LET MY REQUESTS BE MADE KNOWN TO GOD (PHILIPPIANS 4:6). I SUBMIT TO GOD, RESIST SATAN, AND CHOOSE TO FIX MY MIND ON WHATEVER IS RIGHT, PURE, LOVELY, OF GOOD REPUTE, AND WORTHY OF PRAISE, KNOWING THAT THE GOD OF PEACE WILL BE WITH ME (PHILIPPIANS 4:8).

WORD

PART A

WHAT IS ANXIETY?

Welcome to Session 6, which is called "Calm!"

Last time we looked at fear, and today we're going to deal with fear's sibling: anxiety.

The key difference between them is that fear has a definite object—we are frightened of something *specific*—but anxiety does not. It arises from general uncertainty about the future.

We define *anxiety* as "a disturbing unease or apprehension that comes from inappropriate concern about something uncertain." Note that it comes from *inappropriate* concern. It's normal and appropriate to be *nervous* about an exam you're about to take or a plane you're about to catch. That anxiety arises from a particular situation, but it fades away when it's over. That's not what we're talking about in this session.

Facing that violent mob and all the court cases was incredibly stressful, and I became habitually anxious. Many of us experience that. In the UK, one in five adults say they feel anxious most, or all, of the time. And that's when it becomes a problem.

Jesus said bluntly, "Do not be anxious about tomorrow" (Matthew 6:34) and Paul says equally plainly, "Do not be anxious about anything" (Philippians 4:6). And they wouldn't ask us to do something we could not do.

We know that anxiety can have complex causes such as stress or past trauma, so that may sound a bit simplistic. But bear with us. Let's see how living in God's grace can prevent us from being at the mercy of every anxious thought, no matter what circumstances we find ourselves in.

HUMBLE YOURSELF

When Peter wrote to Christians in modern day Turkey who were facing "various trials" that caused them to be anxious, this was his advice: "Humble yourselves, therefore, under God's mighty hand, that he may lift you up in due time. Cast all your anxiety on him because he cares for you" (1 Peter 5:6–7 NIV).

Does God have a mighty hand? Yes! He is all-powerful.

Does He care for you? Yes! He *is* love. He has good plans for you. He *will* lift you up in due time.

Humbling yourself before God is essentially no more than making a choice to believe that these things *are* true and then acting accordingly.

[Rob:] *When my family and I returned from Uganda, on top of the sadness of leaving our lives there, we faced a lot of pressure. We were expecting our third child. We needed to sell our old UK home and find a new home two hundred miles away. Amazingly, a great church in the new area generously offered us a house for three months.*

But then came the news that the house we needed to sell got the worst structural report you can imagine. It was essentially unsellable, so we couldn't afford a new home. I became increasingly anxious; I was being prevented from providing for my family; I genuinely thought we were facing homelessness.

But, my concern was inappropriate, unnecessary even. Because God was still God. His hand was still mighty. He still loved us and was providing for us. A day or two after receiving the structural report . . . one winter's morning and as the sun rose, I was praying as I cycled in to work. I realized I had been trying to run my life myself—again. And I chose right there to humble myself under God's mighty hand, confess my pride in trying to go it alone, trust God for the outcome, and thank Him for how far He had brought us.

Nothing immediately changed in my circumstances, but everything changed in here. The anxiety lifted. It just disappeared, replaced with thankfulness. And, of course, in His perfect timing, God took care of the house and everything else.

[Leisha:] I grew up thinking that I needed to create my own destiny. My life-goal was to achieve a financially comfortable lifestyle. When I became a Christian, the only change I made was that I asked God to bless my plans. My plans!

But God was working on me! I had a reasonably successful career as a university lecturer and also a baking business on the side. I sensed that the Lord was directing me to leave my full-time job and open up a bakery store. Giving up a regular salary with benefits was a huge step. But I handed in my resignation.

And then COVID hit! My manager gave me the option of withdrawing my resignation. But I was so sure that this was what God wanted me to do that I took the plunge.

There were unforeseen expenses. My savings rapidly declined. Things were looking pretty bad. And I became extremely anxious, which caused terrible shoulder pain, neck pain, and insomnia.

I knew I had heard from God so I was confused. Isn't everything supposed to flourish and work well if God told you to do it? That's what I thought at the time, anyway!

One day God helped me to see that the cause of my anxiety was that my goal in life was still the same—to get a comfortable standard of living. And because that felt very uncertain, I was anxious.

I came to understand that God's view of success and God's goal for my life were not the same as mine. He didn't send me here to become a millionaire. And He was using these circumstances to work on areas in me that were not surrendered to Him.

ADOPT GOD'S GOAL FOR YOUR LIFE

Part of humbling yourself before God is making the choice to bring your major life-goals into line with God's goal for you.

What are you hoping to achieve some day? Career success? Getting married and having children? Seeing your children achieve certain things? Having a successful Christian ministry?

Those can be good things. But you can never be sure that they are going to happen. Because they depend on other people or circumstances that are not under your direct control. And that means they will always feel uncertain. So you are setting yourself up for anxiety.

If you get up every morning and head into your day with just one aim—of becoming more and more like Jesus in character—what can stop that from happening? Nothing! So there's no uncertainty, and therefore there's no anxiety.

I realized that God's goal for me was simply to became more like Jesus, and if that happened, then in His eyes I would be extremely successful!

His goal for my life and your life is not so much about what we *do* or *achieve* but what we're *like*.

What if a difficult person attacks me unfairly or gets in my way? Doesn't that stop me achieving God's goal? Or what if I get a really bad health issue? Or my business fails? None of those things can stop you from becoming more and more like Jesus. In fact, if you rely on God and persevere through those difficulties, they will actually *help* you become more and more like Jesus.

Making my vision for success the same as God's has removed uncertainty—because nothing and no one can get in the way of that. This perspective has removed anxiety. No more neck pain, and I sleep well. I can be calm even in a storm.

My business survived and has in fact done well. But that's no longer so important to me. At any moment circumstances could change. And if it fails, the pain of that process can help me toward my new life goal—to be like Jesus. And now I realize that my business is a mission field, which God has called me to.

GET OFF THE FENCE

James describes someone who, in the face of uncertainty and anxiety-causing circumstances, asks God for wisdom but then, instead of persevering through the difficult situations, doubts God and falls back on their own resources. James says, "Such a person is double-minded and unstable in all they do" (James 1:8 NIV).

The Greek word for *anxiety* in the New Testament is a combination of two words meaning "divide" and "mind." Anxiety literally meant being in two minds—constantly going back and forth. Being double-minded. *Like I was between the world's view of success and God's view.* Unless you have made that definite choice to trust God and follow His ways, you'll always be in two minds. And that means you'll be unstable and anxious.

Do you need to come before God and humble yourself? To confess that other things have been more important to you? And to commit yourself to His purpose for you, to become more and more like Jesus? The great news is that you have God's firm promise: He *will* lift you up in due time.

PAUSE FOR THOUGHT 1

OBJECTIVE

To understand how anxiety comes from trying to manage our lives ourselves and causes instability.

1. **Share an occasion when anxiety has caused you to be "double-minded" and led to instability in your walk with God?**

2. **What do you think it looks like in practice to "humble yourself under the mighty hand of God" when you face anxiety?**

PART B

RESOLVING ANXIETY

Peter had something else to say to those who were going through "various trials" that were making them anxious:

"Be alert and of sober mind. Your enemy the devil prowls around like a roaring lion looking for someone to devour. Resist him, standing firm in the faith, because you know that the family of believers throughout the world is undergoing the same kind of sufferings" (1 Peter 5:8–9 NIV).

Perhaps you've never realized that these well-known verses directly follow the other well-known advice to humble ourselves and cast all our anxiety onto God. Our struggle with anxiety isn't just between us and circumstances. Satan is actively trying to get us into anxiety and to exploit the double-mindedness it causes. Anxiety doesn't just raise our blood pressure. It puts us in spiritual danger, too.

At the end of this course, you will go through *The Steps To Experiencing God's Grace*. It's a practical session where you're invited to ask the Holy Spirit to show you the things that are getting in the way of experiencing God's grace. It contains seven steps; the sixth step is called "Exchanging Anxiety For God's Peace." We want to take this opportunity to explain the Biblical principles behind it. Once you know them, you can use them whenever you realize that anxiety has begun to take hold.

1. PRAY

Philippians 4:6 (LSB) says: "Be anxious for nothing, but in everything by prayer and petition with thanksgiving let your requests be made known to God." It starts with prayer. Prayer focuses your mind on God, His character, and His love. Prayer takes our focus off our anxiety and puts our attention on the One who cares for us.

And when you pray, don't forget to give thanks. Thanksgiving focuses your attention on what God has done in the past, and what He's already doing in your current situation.

Apparently the same part of your brain that produces anxiety also generates thanksgiving, so you are literally unable to be thankful and feel anxious at the same time. It only took science 2,000 years to learn what Philippians 4 told us long ago!

2. STATE THE PROBLEM

A problem well-stated is half-solved. For me it was, "I've run out of money." When we're anxious, we struggle to put things into perspective. Ask yourself, will this particular thing that I feel uncertain about matter for eternity? No, I can just start again. Generally speaking, the process of worrying takes a greater toll on us than the worst-case scenario in our thoughts. It's possible to find tremendous relief simply by clarifying the issue and putting it into perspective.

I realized that my business failing wasn't the worst thing that could happen. God would provide. God would lead me in a new direction.

3. FOCUS ON FACTS AND REJECT ASSUMPTIONS

We're anxious because we don't know what is going to happen. And because we don't know, we tend to make assumptions. For many of us, our minds leap to the worst possible outcome, and before we know it, we've convinced ourselves that's what's going to happen! In the vast majority of cases, of course, the worst doesn't happen. So stick to the facts of the situation.

Yes, in my mind I concluded, if my business failed, I was a failure. Which of course isn't true.

4. DETERMINE YOUR RESPONSIBILITIES

Work out prayerfully before God in the situation that is causing your anxiety:

- What is your responsibility?
- What is God's responsibility?
- And what is someone else's responsibility?

The key principle is that you can be responsible only for the things that you have both the *right* and *ability* to control. You are not responsible for what you don't. Generally speaking, the things God has given you the right and ability to control will boil down to things in your own life. And, by the way, if you aren't living a responsible life, then you probably should feel anxious!

My responsibilities were to pay my bills as far as I was able, to continue to be a generous giver despite everything, and to trust God to provide.

Once you've clarified what you're responsible for, then fulfill your responsibilities. Don't just pray about them. You can cast your anxieties onto Jesus, but if you try casting your responsibilities to Him, He will throw them right back to you! *You* might need to forgive someone. *You* might need to put something right. He won't do that for you.

But once you *have* fulfilled your responsibility, you can confidently say, "Now it's up to You, God," and leave everything else with Him.

Then, when you cast your anxiety onto Him, you can be sure that He will play His part. So leave it with Him. Don't pick it up again.

PRACTICAL HELPS

There are some simple practical things we can all do to help our bodies calm down so that we can better focus on God, which will naturally then reduce our anxiety.

- Get outdoors and drink in the beauty of God's creation.

- Take regular physical exercise if you can.

- Control your use of phones, tablets, and other gadgets—constantly flicking from one thing to another gives us the illusion of multitasking or de-stressing but it actually destroys our ability to concentrate and makes us feel anxious.

I realized that my phone was a huge source of anxiety, the sounds of notifications immediately made me anxious. I began turning my phone off in the evenings at a set time and turning it on in the mornings only after I spent time with God and was settled. I also purchased a work phone separate from a personal phone. Then once per week I made sure there was a twenty-four hour period where I would disconnect completely from work devices. This helped me to live a more responsible and balanced life with far less anxiety.

DWELLING IN APPRECIATION

Philippians 4:8–9 says:

Whatever is true, whatever is honorable, whatever is just, whatever is pure, whatever is lovely, whatever is commendable, if there is any excellence, if there is anything worthy of praise, think about these things. What you have learned and received and heard and seen in me—practice these things, and the God of peace will be with you.

Paul is telling us to make a conscious choice about what we focus on. This is not "the power of positive thinking." It's much better than that. We focus on truth. We "marinate" in thanksgiving, letting our hearts become tender.

Praise and worship remind us that God is present, that He's real, and that He's for us. That can calm us like nothing else! There's more in your notes for this session about how you can walk in the power of appreciation.

When we practice dwelling on what is right and lovely and good and worthy of praise, we have God's wonderful promise—the God of peace *will* be with you!

OBJECTIVE

To think about practical measures we could take to combat anxiety.

1. **How have you seen prayer with thanksgiving combat anxiety?**

2. **What practical measures from this section would you like to implement? Share any other practical tips you have learned to overcome anxiety.**

PART C

SEEING GOD AS HE IS

As we've seen, the reason you *can* cast your anxiety onto God is because He cares for you. He is the God of grace. He *is* real, He *is* strong, and He *is* love.

But if you're not sure about Him, or about whether or not He genuinely cares for you, you may bring a concern to Him and ask for His help, but then you'll pick it back up and try to solve it yourself.

You may bring your heavy burden to Him in prayer. But the moment you say "amen," you pick that burden back up again, and carry it through your day.

If you want the truth to set you free, you have to *know* the truth. But here's the thing—Jesus also said, "I *am* the Truth" (John 14:6, emphasis added). Truth is not just a concept. It's a *person*. And you have to know that person.

When I was twenty-one, I married a wonderful young lady named Mandy. She loved me, but I still felt anxious about whether or not she would continue to love me. I wanted to hear every day that she loved me and got frustrated that she could go to sleep without telling me that she loved me. Now, twenty-four years later, that anxiety is gone because I have come to know *her so much better, and that's helped me trust her. This is kind of what Jesus is inviting us to do. He is fully trustworthy, whether we know it or not—so He is*

inviting us to know *it, not just in theory, but to know Him personally.*

What makes it tricky is that the world and the devil paint caricatures of God that keep us from really knowing Him.

Our experiences with our parents and other authority figures also shape our view of our Heavenly Father. So we need to unravel some distorted images if we are to know God as He really is.

Since childhood I've known that I had a good dad—gentle, approachable, affectionate. But he traveled for work and could be gone for weeks at a time. As a young adult, I realized that my image of my Heavenly Father was that of a good God, but a God that wasn't always there for me, was unavailable to me. As if He had ears for others, time for others, but not always for me.

Perhaps your experiences have led you to believe that God is unjust. Or that He's unkind or even cruel. Maybe you feel God is hard to please.

In your notes, you'll find a list of amazing truths called, *"My Father God."*

I am going to read them out to you in an unhurried way. *[Note: you may prefer to get everyone to read these words out loud together—if you do, try to ensure you go slowly.]*

Please focus on the words. You may want to close your eyes to help with that. We want to make space to allow our Father God to speak to your heart, and show you where your past experiences may have given you the wrong idea about Him.

I reject the lie that You, Father God, are distant and uninterested in me.

I choose to believe the truth that You, Father God, are always personally present with me, have plans to give me a hope and a future, and have prepared works in advance specifically for me to do.

I reject the lie that You, Father God, are insensitive and don't know me or care for me.

I choose to believe the truth that You, Father God, are kind and compassionate and know every single thing about me.

I reject the lie that You, Father God, are stern and have placed unrealistic expectations on me.

I choose to believe the truth that You, Father God, have accepted me and are joyfully supportive of me.

I reject the lie that You, Father God, are passive and cold towards me.

I choose to believe the truth that You, Father God, are warm and affectionate towards me.

I reject the lie that You, Father God, are absent or too busy for me.

I choose to believe the truth that You, Father God, are always present and eager to be with me and enable me to be all that You created me to be.

I reject the lie that You, Father God, are impatient or angry with me or have rejected me.

I choose to believe the truth that You, Father God, are patient and slow to anger, and that when You discipline me, it is a proof of Your love and not rejection.

I reject the lie that You, Father God, have been mean, cruel, or abusive to me.

I choose to believe the truth that Satan is mean, cruel, and abusive, but You, Father God, are loving, gentle, and protective.

I reject the lie that You, Father God, are denying me the pleasures of life.

I choose to believe the truth that You, Father God, are the author of life and will lead me into love, joy, and peace when I choose to be filled with Your Spirit.

I reject the lie that You, Father God, are trying to control and manipulate me.

I choose to believe the truth that You, Father God, have set me free, and give me the freedom to make choices and grow in Your grace.

I reject the lie that You, Father God, have condemned me and no longer forgive me.

I choose to believe the truth that You, Father God, have forgiven all my sins and will never use them against me in the future.

I reject the lie that You, Father God, reject me when I fail to live a perfect or sinless life.

I choose to believe the truth that You, Father God, are patient toward me and cleanse me when I fail.

I am the apple of Your eye!

What powerful statements! The lie about God being absent or too busy for me hit home. The truth that God longs to spend time with me was medicine to my soul. Though He holds the entire universe in place, directs history, and cares for every living being, He is never too busy for *me*.

Is there a place where the words seem to stick in your throat? Bring those to Jesus. Ask Him where He was in those times when He seemed less than kind and compassionate or when He seemed absent or uninvolved, and wait for His response.

If you realize you've had a faulty understanding of God, reading this list out loud every day for six weeks or so can help dramatically.

Tough times don't last forever. The God of grace will lift us up in due time. That's why we can flip things over to see trials and tribulations that stir up anxiety as "spiritual exercises." Because resisting anxiety and pressing into Christ builds up spiritual muscle. You probably know that to build muscle, you must first damage the existing muscle. Only then does the body form new protein muscle strands that increase in thickness and number.

So let me say to you, as Jesus said to the stormy sea, "Hush, be still" (Mark 4:39 NASB). You genuinely can cast your anxiety onto the God who is present and powerful, and leave it with Him because He does care for you. Be calm, even in the middle of the storms that you will inevitably pass through.

REFLECT

Introduction

Take a look at that list of truths about our Father God. Read them out loud if possible. Look up the Bible references of any that you are not sure about.

Reflection

Which truth about your Father God is most meaningful to you? How has your view of God been conditioned by experiences of your own father? Ask God to show you where He was in those times when He seemed less than kind and compassionate, or when He seemed absent or uninvolved, and wait for His response. Thank Him for who He is and for being a perfect Father to you.

> CONCLUDING THE SESSION

Remind participants about "Daily Nuggets Of Grace," the devotional that accompanies this course that can be accessed on the YouVersion Bible App, *The Wonder Of Grace* introductory videos, and *The Grace Connection*, the book that accompanies *The Grace Course*.

If you have a date for an Away Day to go through *The Steps To Experiencing God's Grace*, ensure that participants have it in their calendars.

Close in prayer.

> MY FATHER GOD

I reject the lie that You, Father God, are distant and uninterested in me.

I choose to believe the truth that You, Father God, are always personally present with me, have plans to give me a hope and a future, and have prepared works in advance specifically for me to do.

(Psalm 139:1–18; Matthew 28:20, Jeremiah 29:11, Ephesians 2:10)

I reject the lie that You, Father God, are insensitive and don't know me or care for me.

I choose to believe the truth that You, Father God, are kind and compassionate and know every single thing about me.

(Psalm 103:8–14; 1 John 3:1–3; Hebrews 4:12–13)

I reject the lie that You, Father God, are stern and have placed unrealistic expectations on me.

I choose to believe the truth that You, Father God, have accepted me and are joyfully supportive of me.

(Romans 15:27; Zephaniah 3:17))

I reject the lie that You, Father God, are passive and cold towards me.

I choose to believe the truth that You, Father God, are warm and affectionate towards me.

(Isaiah 40:11; Hosea 11:3–4)

I reject the lie that You, Father God, are absent or too busy for me.

I choose to believe the truth that You, Father God, are always present and eager to be with me and enable me to be all that You created me to be.

(Philippians 1:6; Hebrews 13:5)

I reject the lie that You, Father God, are impatient or angry with me or have rejected me.

I choose to believe the truth that You, Father God, are patient and slow to anger, and that when You discipline me, it is a proof of Your love and not rejection.

(Exodus 34:6; Romans 2:4; Hebrews 12:5–11)

I reject the lie that You, Father God, have been mean, cruel, or abusive to me.

I choose to believe the truth that Satan is mean, cruel, and abusive, but You, Father God, are loving, gentle, and protective.

(Psalm 18:2; Matthew 11:28–30; Ephesians 6:10–18)

I reject the lie that You, Father God, are denying me the pleasures of life.

I choose to believe the truth that You, Father God, are the author of life and will lead me into love, joy, and peace when I choose to be filled with Your Spirit.

(Lamentations 3:22–23; Galatians 5:22–24)

I reject the lie that You, Father God, are trying to control and manipulate me.

I choose to believe the truth that You, Father God, have set me free and give me the freedom to make choices and grow in Your grace.

(Galatians 5:1; Hebrews 4:15–16)

I reject the lie that You, Father God, have condemned me and no longer forgive me.

I choose to believe the truth that You, Father God, have forgiven all my sins and will never use them against me in the future.

(Jeremiah 31:31–34; Romans 8:1)

I reject the lie that You, Father God, reject me when I fail to live a perfect or sinless life.

I choose to believe the truth that You, Father God, are patient towards me and cleanse me when I fail.

(Proverbs 24:16; 1 John 1:7–2:2)

I AM THE APPLE OF YOUR EYE!

(Deuteronomy 32:9–10)

> PHYSICAL TIPS TO COMBAT ANXIETY

The major way to combat anxiety is through the Biblical principles outlined in this session but there are some other things that can help, too. God has made our physical bodies to an incredible design that includes some built-in ways to counter anxiety. You may sometimes find yourself subconsciously massaging your arms or rubbing your face—these are small practices that are helping calm your body down.

Here are some other practices you can do:

- Belly breathing—slow and low. This helps deactivate the fight or flight response.

- Inhale to the count of four letting your diaphragm expand, hold to the count of four, exhale to the count of four and say a Bible verse, perhaps Psalm 56:3, "When I am afraid, I will trust in You" (LSB). Then pause and count to four. Repeat three times.

- You could say a name of God like "Lord Jesus" as you inhale, and a Bible verse prayer as you exhale, eg "Help me to be still and know that you are God" (see Psalm 46:10).

Or you could make a simple affirmation, eg "I breathe in your peace, I breathe out your praise."

Take part in worship as the Bible continually exhorts us to: "Let us sing, let us shout to the God of our salvation, let us worship and bow down, let us exalt His name together, let us raise our hearts and hands toward God in heaven" (see Psalm 95). Dr. Richard Smith, head of the Mercy Hospital Neuroscience Institute, found that participatory worship brings about a decrease in blood pressure, a slower pulse, and a reduction in anger and depression.

Tense and then release various muscle groups from your head to your toes. This is something you can do discreetly if a difficult situation arises.

Try yawning. Yawning signals to your body that it is time to quiet and rest. Turn your head to the left, yaw—and then the opposite way and yawn. The result is that more oxygen flows to the brain. One article called it the "fastest way to hack mental stress and gain focus."[1]

Laugh and play. "A merry heart is like good medicine" (Proverbs 17: 22. In Proverbs 8:31, we find God rejoicing in His creation and taking delight in the human beings He created. *John Gill's Exposition of the Bible* says that the word chosen indicates that "it was a kind of sport or play unto him." In other words, it is not just okay to play, but God is actually the author of play.

Physical exercise works wonders. Strenuous exercise releases endorphins which relieve pain and create a sense of well-being. Walking at a little slower pace gives us time to drink in God's beauty in creation.

---

1 Josiah Hultgren, "Yawning is The Fastest Way to Hack Mental Stress and Focus," June 20, 2016, Medium.com, retrieved November 20, 2023, https://medium.com/mindfullyalive/yawning-is-the-fastest-way-to-hack-mental-stress-and-focus-f693edc9f55e.

> DWELLING IN APPRECIATION

When we practice dwelling in appreciation of God, His character, His love, and His works, it changes us. We'll know the true awe and wonder of God—what the Bible calls "fearing the Lord"—and won't be in fear of anything or anyone at all (see Psalm 130:4).

It's not so much about making a list of things you're thankful for but taking time with Him and, as Paul describes in Philippians 4:8–9, **dwelling on** "whatever is true, whatever is honorable, whatever is rjust, whatever is pure, whatever is lovely, whatever is commendable, if there is any excellence, if there is anything worthy of praise."

Here is an approach we recommend that will help you develop a lifestyle of praise and worship that springs from appreciation. You may well find it life-changing!

DRAW NEAR

"Enter His gates with thanksgiving and His courts with praise" (Psalm 100:4). **Draw near** to His presence through thanksgiving and praise.

DWELL

Dwell on these things. Marinate in thanksgiving. Describing in detail to God what you noticed, liked, and appreciated about Him or His works. How did you feel physically as you appreciated Him? Let your heart become tender.

PRACTICE

Practice dwelling—because practice is definitely required! And we have God's wonderful promise: the God of peace will be with you! So do this on a regular basis. It can be very helpful to **build an appreciation file** full of appreciation memories with God. Files help you to bring things to mind readily. These memories will help you make the choice to trust in God, who is the Truth, when circumstances tell you to doubt Him.

LISTEN FOR HIS VOICE

The practice of appreciating God allows us to hear the voice of God. Psalm 95 begins by saying, "O come, let us sing for joy into the Lᴏʀᴅ, let us shout joyfully to the rock of our salvation. Let us come before His presence with thanksgiving, let us shout joyfully to Him with psalms." Then it goes on to say (verse 7), "Today if you would hear His voice, do not harden your hearts" (verses 7–8 ɴᴀꜱʙ1995). Dwelling in appreciation prepares the way to hear God's voice, so **listen for His voice**.

session **07**

FRUITFUL!

OBJECTIVE

To help us bear more and more fruit
as disciples of Jesus by resting in God,
trusting in His ways, and offering our
whole selves to Him as living sacrifices.

LEADER'S NOTES

This session should hammer the final nail into the coffin for any idea that this course is about "cheap grace." It brings home the uncomfortable truth that the gateway to fruitfulness is brokenness.

Some will struggle to understand that God could bring into our lives events that are painful and hard. It's important to help them see that if God does that, it is for our ultimate good and for the good of His purposes.

It's also important not to let people think that every bad thing that happens is from God. We must not ignore the effects of sin and the fact that we have an enemy, Satan. But God in His grace will work for our good in every situation, whatever its cause.

By definition, everyone in fruitful ministry has been through some breaking experiences, so do try to share your own stories. If you are teaching this yourself, you may find it helpful to show the portions from the video presentation which feature stories from others.

SMALL GROUP TIMINGS

The following plan is designed to help those leading the course in small groups. It assumes a meeting of around ninety minutes in length, and suggests how long each part of the session should last, with an indication of cumulative elapsed time. You will find a time plan in each session. The second column shows the time allocated to each individual element in minutes and seconds. The third column shows the total elapsed time in hours and minutes.

Session 7	Minutes:Seconds	Hours:Minutes
Welcome, Focus, Connect	13:00	00:13
Word Part A	12:30	00:25
Pause For Thought 1	12:30	00:38
Word Part B	12:00	00:50
Pause For Thought 2	14:00	01:04
Word Part C	12:00	01:16
Reflect	14:00	01:30

The time allocated for the Word sections is based on the length of the corresponding section of the videos. Registered users of the course can download an Excel spreadsheet with these timings. Simply enter your own start time, adjust the length of the various components if desired and you will have a customized plan for your session.

FOCUS VERSE

"I am the vine, you are the branches. Whoever abides in me and I in him, he it is that bears much fruit, for apart from me you can do nothing."

John 15:5

FOCUS TRUTH

If we want to be fruitful, our focus needs to be not on bearing fruit but on staying close to Jesus and humbling ourselves to live according to God's ways as revealed in the Bible.

CONNECT

Some people are said to have a "green thumb" because of their success in growing plants. What is your track record in this area?

In John 15, Jesus compares Himself to a vine, and us to branches of that vine. How does it encourage you to know that He also says that Father God is the gardener?

If you watched *The Wonder Of Grace* introductory video for this session, what was the main thing that struck you?

Was there anything in the YouVersion "Daily Nuggets Of Grace" that especially made you think?

PRAYER & DECLARATION

In every session, we want to encourage people to pray out loud and to make a declaration out loud together. A prayer is addressed to God while a declaration is spoken out to the spiritual world in general.

Encourage people to make their declaration boldly!

Our Father, Your Kingdom come! Your will be done! I repent of striving in my own strength to bring about Your Kingdom purposes. Please teach me to depend upon the power of Your Life within me. I desire to live a "grace-rest" life, trusting You with all my heart and not leaning on my own understanding, submitting to You, knowing that You will make my paths straight (Proverbs 3:5–6). I know that all discipline seems not to be joyful, but sorrowful; yet to those who have been trained by it, afterwards it yields the peaceful fruit of righteousness (Hebrews 12:5,6,11). Amen.

I AM A BRANCH OF THE TRUE VINE, JESUS, A CHANNEL OF HIS LIFE. I CHOOSE TO REMAIN IN HIM SO THAT I CAN BEAR MUCH FRUIT. NO ONE CAN TAKE ME OUT OF HIS HANDS. I AM FREE FROM THE POWER OF SIN, THE POWER OF SATAN AND THE POWER OF DEATH. FREE TO MAKE GOOD CHOICES. I CHOOSE TO LAY DOWN EVERYTHING AT GOD'S FEET—MY HEALTH, MY PLANS, MY MONEY, MY FAMILY, MY MINISTRY AND MY FUTURE. I CHOOSE TO MAKE JESUS MY KING—AND MY VERY LIFE.

WORD

PART A

HOW TO BEAR FRUIT

Welcome to the seventh session of *The Grace Course* which is called "Fruitful!" This is where we start to look farther ahead to the rest of our lives and how we can become even more fruitful disciples of Jesus.

That's what I always wanted, that's what I spent so long striving for—and it didn't work. If only Jesus could tell me exactly how to bear fruit—oh wait, He did! Towards the end of His earthly life, Jesus said this:

> "I am the true vine, and my Father is the gardener. He cuts off every branch in me that bears no fruit, while every branch that does bear fruit he prunes so that it will be even more fruitful. You are already clean because of the word I have spoken to you. Remain in me, as I also remain in you. No branch can bear fruit by itself; it must remain in the vine. Neither can you bear fruit unless you remain in me. I am the vine; you are the branches. If you remain in me and I in you, you *will* bear much fruit; apart from me you can do nothing." (John 15:1–5 NIV)

So, what is a branch's one responsibility?

Instinctively you might say, "Well, to bear fruit of course!"

Nope. It's more fundamental than that. If you venture into a vineyard, you'll never, ever hear grunting and groaning as the branches strain to pop out grapes. The branches don't need to strain. If they're connected to the vine, they don't have to try. It just happens. So our one responsibility is to "remain" in Jesus. To stay connected to

Him. To keep close to Him. If you do that, you enter a life of "grace-rest" where, paradoxically, you *will* bear lots of fruit.

Jesus said another surprising thing: "The Son can do nothing by himself; he can do only what he sees his Father doing" (John 5:19 NIV).

Even though He was God, He wasn't operating out of His "God-ness." But He was modeling how *we* are to live. He simply focused on being in a loving relationship with the Father. Then He saw what the Father was doing and joined in.

Being on the leadership team of that ministry in Uganda, I used to get so anxious—particularly about the finance we needed, the people who were dependent on our programs being successful—it used to keep me awake at night. Sometimes we'd raise lots of money, other times . . . not. But you know, it was the "not" times that I'm most thankful for. Coming to the end of my own resources meant I knew—really knew—that I can do nothing unless I depend totally on Jesus and let Him do it.

If you *strain* to bear fruit, to achieve some kind of success—a ministry position or some other target—it just doesn't work.

Why? Because you remove yourself from a grace-based trust in Jesus where you know that you can do nothing apart from Him. And instead, you put yourself into a law-based system of anxious performance, where everything depends on you. And you just can't make it *all* happen.

Whenever I was asked to do a task at church, I felt like the onus was on me to perform and almost make myself good enough. I would go into intense preparation mode trying to get every single thing absolutely right with no room for error. And no room for relying on Jesus!

One day I felt the Holy Spirit prompting my heart to lead a small group through a study on the topic of relationships and dating. My reaction was "No Sah! (that's Jamaican for no way). I have a failed marriage. I have no credentials for this!"

Then I distinctly remember hearing a small voice say, "The Holy Spirit is your credential." I felt totally out of my depth, but I went ahead and I did it. And God really worked.

It turned out that God didn't need my skills or lack thereof. He just wanted me to lean in to His direction and depend on Him.

PRINCIPLE 1: APART FROM JESUS WE CAN DO *NOTHING*

Our first principle for bearing fruit is this: apart from Jesus we can do nothing.

We naturally think that it all comes down to our own efforts. And we therefore risk burning out or being overwhelmed. Most of us have to learn this the hard way. To help us learn, God will often allow us to struggle under the burden of trying to do it ourselves.

If *you* are feeling that pressure, Jesus makes you an offer today:

> "Come to me, all who labor and are heavy laden, and I will give you rest. Take my yoke upon you, and learn from me, for I am gentle and lowly in heart, and you will find rest for your souls. For my yoke is easy, and my burden is light." (Matthew 11:28–30)

What an amazing statement of grace! This verse has been a constant reminder to me throughout my Christian journey from the day of my baptism and every time since then that I have become overwhelmed. I have come to realize that God genuinely offers me a yoke that is easy and a burden that is light. And most importantly, rest for our soul. That doesn't mean lying around doing nothing. If it did, it wouldn't be a picture of two oxen plowing a field. It's an internal rest that is based on faith and dependence on God. It means that you truly follow His lead and go at His pace.

TRUST GOD, BEAR FRUIT

When God made the world He worked for six days and then rested on the seventh. God didn't go off for a nap—that's not the sense of the original Hebrew words at all. God "rested" because His all-powerful reign over the universe began and all was as it should be.

Adam was created on day six, so the first full day of his life was that day of rest, a day of *connecting* with God, *knowing* that God was in charge, and *actively trusting* Him.

So first we rest in God's reality and provision, and then we work. We learn to trust God, then we bear fruit.

And yet so much of our lives are spent the other way around—we wear ourselves out, and then we rest to recover. If you're anything like me, I can find myself working harder and harder, and in some desperation praying, "Oh Lord, bless the work of my hands and I'll trust You more!"

When all along, it's supposed to be the other way around. Trust God, then bear fruit.

Apart from Jesus, we can do *nothing*. Now, you can get out of bed, eat breakfast, brush your teeth, get dressed, go to work, make a living, raise a family, grow old, retire, and die without Jesus. But you can do nothing of *eternal* value unless it comes out of resting in *His* ability and staying connected to Him.

It's not enough to know Jesus as Savior. It's not even enough to know Him as King. We need to come to realize that He is, as Paul puts it, our very Life (see Colossians 3:4).

When we "get" this, it's incredibly liberating. You're free to leave behind that false motivator of pride that leads to anxious performance. You know that you don't need to try to control events or people. You can trust God to take care of the things that are outside your control. You come to see that He really does work in all things for your good (Romans 8:28).

PAUSE FOR THOUGHT 1

OBJECTIVE

To begin to explore the concept of complete dependence on the Father.

1. **Read John 5:19–20. In what ways did Jesus' life on earth demonstrate His complete dependence upon the Father?**

2. **In what ways might our lives look different if we depended completely on God?**

PART B

PRINCIPLE 2: FRUITFULNESS COMES ONLY WHEN WE SUBMIT TO GOD AND DO WHAT HE SAYS

When Mandy and I moved to a remote area of Northern Nigeria, we were just twenty-three years old, married for two years, and didn't speak the Tsuva'di language at all. People thought we were crazy. Maybe we were! But we were sure God had called us—His Word clearly shows His love for the nations and tells us to go make disciples—so we went.

Because we were so young and inexperienced, and this was all so overwhelming, we knew we couldn't do it. That drove us to depend totally on God. He didn't need us. But like a loving father allows a child to "help" him with a task, even though it takes longer and will probably need redoing, our Heavenly Father just loves to work through us.

One of the highlights of my life, come two years later, watching people in our village be baptized. They had lived in complete darkness and had never once heard Jesus' name, and now they were publicly declaring, "I belong to God."

I take no credit whatsoever because I know what I'm like, and I know I couldn't make this happen. God loves to take us way beyond our own abilities and then to do amazing things so that it's obvious that the fruit comes by His grace and not by our efforts.

One day, God revealed to Simon Peter, one of Jesus' disciples, just who Jesus was. The Son of God. An incredible revelation. Seizing the moment, Jesus begins to explain even more of God's plans, including that He is going to have to suffer and die.

But Peter interrupts Him and tells Him that He can't possibly be right.

Think about that. Peter has just understood that He's face-to-face with God Himself. And his response is to tell the Creator of the Universe that He's got it all wrong. How arrogant can you get?

Adam's downfall came when Satan persuaded him that he, *too*, knew better than God. And all of us are prone to do exactly the same thing that Adam and Peter did.

God says, "As the heavens are higher than the earth, so are my ways higher than your ways and my thoughts than your thoughts" (Isaiah 55:9).

Our finite minds can never fully grasp who God is and how He works. That's why Augustine said "If you understand, it is not God," because He is so different from us. He breaks our paradigms at every turn.

> Trust in the LORD with all your heart and lean not on your own understanding; in all your ways submit to him, and he will make your paths straight. (Proverbs 3:5–6 NIV)

Instead of acting out of pride and trusting our own understanding, our worldview, or our past experiences, we need to learn to trust what God says. He promises that, when we do, He will "make our paths straight." We can expect our lives to be fruitful.

Our second principle is that fruitfulness comes only when we submit to God and what He says, when we set aside our pride and choose to humble ourselves before Him.

THE BIBLE REVEALS GOD'S WAYS

How do we know what God says? Well, He's revealed in the Bible what He's like, how He's set up the world, and our part in His plans.

And that's why much of Satan's attack is directed at how people see the Bible. He wants you not to take it seriously. Not to read it for yourself. Not to spend that time with God each day where you humble yourself before Him and His Word. To make us think, like Simon Peter, that we know better than God.

Have you heard people say things like, "I only trust the red text in the Bible," or "I don't get the Old Testament, so I just skip it"?

Paul told Timothy, "The Spirit clearly says that in later times [which is now!] some will abandon the faith and follow deceiving spirits and things taught by demons" (1 Timothy 4:1 NIV).

He's talking about people who claim to be Christians following the teaching of demons. So don't be surprised if you hear Christian teachers implying that the Bible doesn't say what it plainly does say.

Satan used the phrase, "Did God *really* say?" (Genesis 3:1). And he uses that line with us, too. Satan even quoted Bible verses and twisted their meaning. History is full of examples of people being led astray by fraudulent arguments and shady theology.

HUMBLING OURSELVES BEFORE GOD AND HIS WORD

Does that make the Bible an unreliable guide? Not at all. It's totally consistent in what it says. And God promises to guide you into all truth by His Spirit. If you approach His Word with a humble, teachable spirit, you *will* understand what He has to say to you.

Please, don't just listen to us or others *talk* about the Bible. Or read Bible study notes only. Read the Bible for yourself.

Take what it says seriously. You can base your life-decisions on God's promises. Don't think they apply to other people but that your problems are different or too big. That's also a form of pride.

Don't come to it with a preconceived idea of what you want it to say, even if your intentions seem good. Focus on what it *actually* says.

I've watched countless Christians read in the Bible that they are holy ones, but totally miss the point that that's who they actually are! Because they've always heard they're sinners. They filter what is written plainly in the Bible through the theology they've been taught. It should be the other way around. Always judge what you've been taught according to the Bible.

And if a passage doesn't make immediate sense, don't gloss over it. Persevere, ask, research, and listen until you understand why the God who is love included it. Try to understand the culture it was written for and don't make it say anything that the original hearers could not have understood from it.

When I come to the Bible looking for specific direction—which option to choose or the way out of a mess—God usually shows me that His priority is different to mine. My Bible reading may not give me the A-B-C answer I seek, but it does remind me how God wants me to live here and now. He's more concerned with my *character* than what I *do*. As I work on my heart, He usually takes care of the specific situation, too, though rarely how I imagined.

Four years ago, my daughter entered a deep, dark spiritual struggle with anorexia. It affected her mental, physical, and spiritual health. Honestly, it was a painful, dark time for our whole family. Things from the Bible that I thought I understood . . . didn't go as I expected. I thought if I just took authority over it in Jesus' name, then my daughter would be well and I could shield my family from this shadow of death. It was a really painful time of wrestling with God and being stretched.

That situation forced me to go beyond my understanding and to dig deep into God's Word. The way I understood God and His purposes—my theology, if you like—changed.

Of course, God never changes. And truth never changes. Our theology, on the other hand, is our attempt to understand God and His truth. As we grow as Christians, our understanding develops and our theology can change.

I thank God that my daughter is walking with the Lord and doing much better, but there are still aspects of this ordeal that I don't understand.

We are totally committed to God's truth as revealed in the Bible. But as long as we are on this earth, we will always be learning more about God and His ways as He reveals them to us through His Word.

OBJECTIVE

To explore how the Bible can be misused.

1. **How can we prevent ourselves from being deceived in our understanding of the Bible?**

2. **How might well-meaning people be tempted to twist the Bible to match their own biases and preferences?**

PART C

PRINCIPLE 3: THE GATEWAY TO FRUITFULNESS IS BROKENNESS

I had a stable job and was highly esteemed in my local church. I was finally feeling like "I got this!" And that was when God told me to do the hard thing of leaving my job and church and removed me from what was familiar.

It seemed like He took away good things but did you notice this phrase in the passage earlier: "Every branch that *does* bear fruit he prunes so that it will be even more fruitful" (John 15:2 NIV, emphasis added). That doesn't sound like much fun. Pruning is downright painful. But it's done to those who are already bearing fruit so that they will bear even more.

I now know that He placed me in a new church and a new business to do something even better: He developed my character and helped me become more like Jesus.

And God is continually working to cut away our self-centeredness, self-reliance and pride. We're told that even Jesus "learned obedience through what he suffered" (Hebrews 5:8).

That's why our third principle is that the gateway to fruitfulness is brokenness.

In every season of hardship—whether instability, persecution, conflict, family issues, whatever twist suffering has taken—I know that I have been refined and pruned so I can bear more fruit. Surprisingly, I've even seen fruit *while* I was feeling broken.

My first experience of doing this kind of thing was as a presenter on the *Freedom In Christ Course*. At the time, I was still reeling from three transatlantic moves in three years. And I told that story in real time in front of an audience and seven cameras. I felt weak and vulnerable. However, not only am I now confident that brokenness is the gateway to fruitfulness, I saw that my stories of pain and suffering and God's grace in their midst are the best gifts I have to offer to others.

In Hebrews 12, the writer says,

> All discipline for the moment seems not to be joyful, but sorrowful; yet to those who have been trained by it, afterwards it yields the peaceful fruit of righteousness. (Hebrews 12:11 NASB1995)

God isn't the cause of every difficulty. But He will use every difficulty for our good—even my divorce and difficult seasons in business when I ran out of money. He never wastes any experience. Tough times are where we learn to trust Him.

When God gave Paul a difficult situation specifically to prevent him from becoming proud, understandably Paul asked Him to take it away. Three times. But God said, "My grace is sufficient for you, for my power is made perfect in weakness" (2 Corinthians 12:9).

No one's saying that we should enjoy difficulties. But they aren't always things to be prayed out of the way.

King David wrote in Psalm 131:1 (NIV):

> My heart is not proud, O LORD, my eyes are not haughty; I do not concern myself with great matters or things too wonderful for me.

This is *King* David. He *does* deal with "great matters." He makes life and death decisions every day. But here he simply recognizes that if he thought he could do them in his own strength, it would be pride. Then he says, "No, right now I am calm and quiet, like a child after nursing, content in its mother's arms" (Psalm 131:2 ERV).

Deep inside of all of us, there's a part that cries out restlessly like a hungry infant. It can be from shame, guilt, fear, fleshly urges, or pride.

But, by persevering through extreme difficulties when King Saul was hunting him down, David learned to rest in God. To allow God alone to satisfy him. This is the "peaceful fruit of righteousness" (Hebrews 12:11). It comes when we go through that gateway of brokenness and we rest in God and take Him at His Word.

Let's review our three counterintuitive grace principles for fruitfulness:

- Apart from Jesus we can do *nothing*.
- Fruitfulness comes *only* when we submit to God and do what He says
- The gateway to fruitfulness is brokenness.

BECOME A LIVING SACRIFICE

Do you still want to be an even more fruitful disciple of Jesus?

If you do, Paul suggests something specific you can do as a response to God's grace:

> I urge you, brothers and sisters, in view of God's mercy, to offer your bodies as a living sacrifice, holy and pleasing to God (Romans 12:1 NIV).

The idea of a live animal being placed on an altar as a *living* sacrifice is amusing—because it can jump up and run away!

But think about the hours that Jesus hung on the cross in incredible agony, every breath a massive, painful effort, until His heart burst from the strain. A literal living sacrifice. He could have left at any moment. He was God. But He chose not to. And I am eternally thankful He made that choice.

Paul says that making ourselves a living sacrifice is a response to God's mercy. So let's remind ourselves of some of the things we now know about God's grace:

Jesus became a sacrifice for you, paying an unimaginable price so that you are now declared completely innocent.

Jesus became sin on your behalf, and you became the righteousness of God, a holy one.

You are now safe and secure. No one can take you out of His hands. And His love can drive out every unhealthy fear.

You can cast all your anxiety on Him and walk in peace because He cares for you.

You are genuinely free. Free from the power of sin, the power of Satan, and the power of death. Free to make good choices.

You need only focus on remaining in Him in order to bear lots of fruit.

You are now secure enough in who you are in Christ to humble yourself before God and before others. With no need to try to control events or people.

You know that you can do absolutely nothing in your own strength but that He can do absolutely anything through you.

So here you are, a son or daughter of the King of Kings, standing there dressed in your rich robe, your ring of authority, and your sandals.

And God Himself is looking at you with eyes of pure love and delight.

You might say, "God, thank You so much. I really do want to be even more fruitful. What do You want me to do for You?" I suspect His response might be, "There are things for you to do. But what I really want is *you*. All of you"

Can I join Paul and urge you to climb onto that altar as a living sacrifice? To lay down everything at His feet—your health, your plans, your money, your family, your ministry, your future? To make Jesus your King—and your very Life?

It's okay to come like the younger son in complete weakness and just collapse. God will run to you and embrace you. He'll never abandon you. He'll never take you beyond what you can bear as He gives you strength.

Let's pray.

Loving Father God,

Thank You for sending Jesus, Who, being in very nature God, did not consider equality with God something to be used to His own advantage but made Himself nothing and humbled Himself by becoming obedient to death—even death on a cross.

I choose right now to trust in You with all my heart. I deliberately turn away from relying on my own understanding. I submit to You in all my ways, in every part of my life. Thank You that You will make my paths straight.

Thank You for the Bible, Your clear Word to us. I pray that You will help me understand it in all of its wonderful fullness as I come with an open heart ready to hear Your instructions, encouragement, and correction. I refuse to water Your Word down, gloss it over, or try to make it say what I think it should say. Thank You that Your Holy Spirit will lead me into all truth.

Please help me root out the deeply ingrained lies I have believed and replace them with truth so that I may truly be transformed by the renewing of my mind.

As a response to Your grace, I choose here and now to offer You my body and all that I am as a living sacrifice, holy and pleasing to You. This is my true and proper worship.

And I worship You now.

Amen.

REFLECT

Introduction

God was not the cause of all the difficult things you have experienced in your life, but He does promise to work in them and turn them around to good. In this time, cast your mind back to difficult times in your life and ask God to show you how He was working in them.

Reflection

What fruit can you see in your own character or life from those experiences?

Paul said he could be "content with weaknesses, insults, hardships, persecutions, and calamities" (2 Corinthians 12:10). Do you think he really meant that? Tell God how you feel about the gateway to fruitfulness being brokenness.

> CONCLUDING THE SESSION

Remind participants about "Daily Nuggets Of Grace," the devotional that accompanies this course that can be accessed on the YouVersion Bible App, *The Wonder Of Grace* introductory videos, and *The Grace Connection*, the book that accompanies *The Grace Course*.

If you are planning an Away Day to go through *The Steps To Experiencing God's Grace*, it will be coming up soon. You may like to ensure that participants are aware of the details and take a moment to assure them that it is a kind, gentle process just between them and God. No one will be asked to share anything in front of anyone else.

Close in prayer.

FREEDOM
IN CHRIST

session **08**

PEACEMAKER!

OBJECTIVE

To help us understand the crucial role of the Church, the body and Bride of Christ, in God's plans and why a passionate commitment to maintaining the unity of the Spirit in the bond of peace is vital if we are to reach this world for Christ.

LEADER'S NOTES

In this session we major on the importance of unity as the body of Christ. The concept of Christian unity has been devalued in some circles, and we want to emphasize that we do not have in view some kind of "lowest common denominator" compromised statement of beliefs. We are talking about a heart unity based on our identity together in Christ.

Some have seen grace and truth as opposites—as if the more grace we have, the less truth we have and vice versa. Yet John describes Jesus as "full of grace *and* truth" (John 1:14, emphasis added). They are not opposites. They are complementary. We need both 100 percent grace and 100 percent truth; grace that does not compromise truth, and truth that does not compromise grace.

Consider two of the seven churches that Jesus addresses in his seven brief letters in Revelation.

In Revelation 2:1–7, Jesus commends the church in Ephesus for their hard work, their perseverance, and for identifying and removing leaders who were not true apostles. This is a church with an emphasis on truth. It has correct doctrine. Great teaching. Effective discipline.

Like the Ephesians, most of us have been taught that truth is the most important aspect of our faith and that we need to uphold it at all costs. But Jesus' words to them are devastating: "You have abandoned the love you had at first" (verse 4). They have overlooked grace. And He tells them, "Repent, and do the works you did at first" (verse 5).

Among the seven churches, there is just one, the church in Thyatira (Revelation 2:18–29), that Jesus commends for its love. However, as we read on, we discover that the church has also tolerated false teaching along the lines of, "God is love, so He won't mind if we bend the rules." And people had lapsed into idol worship and sexual immorality. In Part C of this session, we quote Jesus' hard words about the consequences for the ringleader:

"Behold, I will throw her onto a sickbed, and those who commit adultery with her I will throw into great tribulation, unless they repent of her works, and I will strike her children dead" (Revelation 2:22–23).

There is a long history of churches thinking they are upholding God's love when in fact they are encouraging people into sin, and of churches thinking that they are upholding God's truth when actually they are just being arrogant and divisive.

How is it possible to have 100 percent grace and 100 percent truth? Let's consider the meaning of those key words to the Biblical writers.

TRUTH

Our concept of truth has been hijacked by Western rationalism which has taught us to see truth as something that we access primarily via the intellect and that stands on its own, regardless of whether we know it or believe it. Objective truth does of course exist, but this is not at all the concept the Biblical writers had in mind when they used the word.

In the Old Testament, the Hebrew word translated "truth" is *emeth* and means "faithful and true." It implies being faithful and true toward somebody else (which is something an objective fact cannot do). It's a relational word.

Similarly when Jesus promises that we will know the truth and that the truth will set us free, He speaks as the One who also says that He *is* the Truth.

Jesus is 100 percent truth in that He is a consistent, living demonstration of the nature and character of God. As we put our trust in Him, we discover in our experience—not just intellectually—that He is always "faithful and true."

Understanding truth primarily as objective fact, however, has caused us to teach that there is a right answer to every issue (and that *we* have it!) and to conclude that unity has to be based on doctrinal agreement. In practice, that has led to pathological disunity.

We absolutely do need good theology, and the truth of God's Word forms the bedrock of *The Grace Course*.

But the real basis for our unity is a person. We unite in Christ who is the Truth.

GRACE

Grace is another relational word which means to give freely to someone who does not deserve it.

Have you ever sent a gift through the mail and never received a thank-you? You worry it hasn't arrived, but you feel nervous to ask in case they just don't like it? Well, in the world of the Biblical writers, if a gift didn't elicit a response, it would imply that it had not been received.

Paul says that God's kindness leads us to repentance (Romans 2:4). God's grace assures us of His love for us no matter what we do. But if that doesn't move us to respond to Him in repentance, and by reaffirming our allegiance to Him, with a corresponding change in our behavior, then we have not actually received it.

So tolerating sin, like the church in Thyatira did, is not grace. Neither is sentimental love that demands nothing and does not challenge sin.

There is much more we could say but the apostle Paul says it far better than we could:

> Make every effort to keep the unity of the Spirit through the bond of peace. There is one body and one Spirit, just as you were called to one hope when you were called; one Lord, one faith, one baptism; one God and Father of all, who is over all and through all and in all. (Ephesians 4:3–6 NIV)

SMALL GROUP TIMINGS

The following plan is designed to help those leading the course in small groups. It assumes a meeting of around ninety minutes in length, and suggests how long each part of the session should last, with an indication of cumulative elapsed time. You will find a time plan in each session. The second column shows the time allocated to each individual element in minutes and seconds. The third column shows the total elapsed time in hours and minutes.

Session 8	Minutes:Seconds	Hours:Minutes
Welcome, Focus, Connect	13:00	00:13
Word Part A	13:30	00:26
Pause For Thought 1	12:30	00:39
Word Part B	10:00	00:49
Pause For Thought 2	14:00	01:03
Word Part C	13:00	01:16
Reflect	14:00	01:30

The time allocated for the Word sections is based on the length of the corresponding section of the videos. Registered users of the course can download an Excel spreadsheet with these timings. Simply enter your own start time, adjust the length of the various components if desired and you will have a customized plan for your session.

FOCUS VERSE

"By this all people will know that you are my disciples, if you have love for one another."

John 13:35

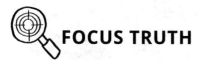

FOCUS TRUTH

Unity is key to exercising the spiritual authority to disciple the nations that Jesus delegated to us.

CONNECT

If you were writing a book about your life, what would you like the title of the next chapter to be?

Read Psalm 133:

> How good and pleasant it is when God's people live together in unity! It is like precious oil poured on the head, running down on the beard, running down on Aaron's beard, down on the collar of his robe. It is as if the dew of Hermon were falling on Mount Zion. For there the LORD bestows his blessing, even life forevermore. (NIV)

Where have you seen unity bring blessing?

If you watched *The Wonder Of Grace* introductory video for this session, what was the main thing that struck you?

Was there anything in the YouVersion "Daily Nuggets Of Grace" that especially made you think?

PRAYER & DECLARATION

In every session, we want to encourage people to pray out loud and to make a declaration out loud together. A prayer is addressed to God while a declaration is spoken out to the spiritual world in general.

Encourage people to make their declaration boldly!

Dear Heavenly Father, thank You for the promise in Psalm 133 that says that it's in unity that You bestow Your blessing, life forevermore. As children of God living out of our identity in Christ, we desire to be peacemakers. Please help us to learn to forgive relentlessly and show us how to maintain the unity of the Spirit in the bond of peace (Ephesians 4:3). In Jesus' mighty name we pray. Amen.

IN THE NAME OF JESUS, WE HUMBLE OURSELVES BEFORE GOD AND BEFORE OUR BROTHERS AND SISTERS IN CHRIST. WE TAKE OUR STAND AGAINST EVERY ENEMY OF HIS THAT WOULD BRING DISUNITY OR CONFUSION AND WE COMMAND THEM TO LEAVE US NOW.

○ WORD

PART A

JESUS DELEGATES SPIRITUAL AUTHORITY TO US

Welcome to Session 8, "Peacemaker!"

Well, I'd read all the books and done all the training. And it was with great excitement that I went to Uganda to "Go and make disciples" (Matthew 28:19 niv). I joined a fantastic team and helped develop some great outreach programs. But the fruit was limited, to say the least, so I tried harder—but the harder I tried, the less fruit I saw. I definitely needed to "get" that grace-rest we talked about last session. But was there more than that going on?

Jesus doesn't *just* command us to go and make disciples. He starts by stating a crucial prerequisite: "All authority in heaven and on earth has been given to me" (Matthew 28:18).

Only on that basis, does He then go on to say: "*Therefore*, go and make disciples . . ."

At the cross Jesus "disarmed the powers and authorities, [and] he made a public spectacle of them" (Colossians 2:15 niv). He is now seated at the right hand of the Father far above every demonic power and authority. And in this statement He delegates that spiritual authority to us. Why? Specifically in order to disciple the nations.

My Western worldview had led me to totally misunderstand the spiritual world. I knew it was real, but to be honest I was scared of it, so I avoided it. Even though I'd read the words

hundreds of time, I didn't really get why Jesus was talking about authority here. And I certainly didn't understand how to exercise authority.

Why, would you say, aren't more people out there turning to Jesus? Paul explains it clearly in another verse that we tend to gloss over. He says it's because Satan "has blinded the minds of the unbelievers" so that they just can't see the light of the gospel (2 Corinthians 4:4).

If that's the reason, just telling them the gospel won't work. They can't see it. How can we counteract this spiritual problem? With the spiritual authority over Satan that Jesus has delegated to us.

How do we activate that? We often overlook a clear but counterintuitive fact that Jesus tells us:

> "By this all people will know that you are my disciples, *if you have love for one another*." (John 13:35, emphasis added)

And the one thing Jesus chose to pray for us, who come after His original disciples, is that we would all be one, just as He and the Father are one. Why? "'So that the world may believe that you have sent me'" (John 17:21).

Psalm 133 tells us that it is in unity that "the Lord has commanded the blessing, life forevermore." When we love each other, we walk in that blessing; it's a delegated authority, a spiritual power. And Satan cannot resist it.

Look at the book of Acts where the early Church had no real resources but was totally united. Thousands of people at a time had their eyes opened to the light of the gospel and responded to it. Why not in your local area, too?

Together we are God's chosen instrument to disciple the nations. There is no Plan B.

THE BODY OF CHRIST

That's why the New Testament continually urges us to be united and talks of us as "the body of Christ." It's more than just a metaphor. If you think about it, we are the actual flesh and blood, the arms and legs, through whom God works in the world.

As individual Christians on our own, we're like a dismembered leg or a single eye—no use whatsoever without the rest of the body. You can't be fruitful on your own, even if you're listening to the best spiritual podcasts.

In Acts, Luke used a word no fewer than ten times to describe unity. It's usually translated as "with one mind" but its literal sense is "with one passion."

Unity is "a shared *passion* for God and for His purposes that is so strong it overrides our different preferences and opinions."

I wonder, are you starting to get at least a little bit passionate about unity because of its crucial importance in reaching this world for Christ?

I've had the privilege of meeting and worshiping regularly with other Christians from all traditions. You might think filling a room full of people from different denominations is a sure recipe for a bun-fight, but the reverse was true. We had the most amazing and powerful times of healing and renewal. How? What was the secret? We all had this passion to fix our eyes on Jesus, and our differences just faded to insignificance.

Jesus said, "Blessed are the peacemakers, for they will be called children of God" (Matthew 5:9 NIV). Being peacemakers and children of God are two inseparable sides of a coin. If you are a child of God, living out of your identity in Christ, you will be a peacemaker.

FIND YOUR PLACE IN THE BODY

So first things first. If you're not already part of a local church fellowship, can we encourage you to join one?

When I first went off to college, I remember "touring" the different local churches. I approached it a bit like choosing a sports club or a restaurant—you know, "Which church is best for me, which ticks my boxes?"

The question should, of course, be "Where do *You* want me to serve You, Lord?" He may place you somewhere unexpected, but He knows where your unique contribution will work best.

Find the place that God has for you in that body. And if He hasn't made you the leader, follow those whom God has chosen to lead. All of us sometimes think that we know better than our leaders. But unless they're clearly overstepping the bounds of their authority or are in obvious sin, it's our job to encourage and support them—warts and all.

When you know that God Himself has specifically called you to a unique role in a particular part of His body, you are much more likely to persevere when it gets tough. And it will.

As a pastor's wife, I was shocked when the hardest blows came from inside the church rather than from the world. I remember telling Jesus, "if this is the Church, I want nothing to do with it." Jesus responded, "Nancy, do you love Me? Feed My lambs." He knew I'd begun to see them not as lambs but as vampire bats. "Nancy, do you love Me? Take care of My sheep." So because I love Jesus, I choose to love the Church, too.

No, being part of a church is not easy. But it is essential. Satan understands the power of our unity and will relentlessly tempt us into disunity. So we'll always experience people who see things differently, make mistakes, attack us, offend us, or just really get up our nose.

There's a great biblical principle: "If it is possible, as far as it depends on you, live at peace with everyone" (Romans 12:18 NIV).

We are to do what is in our power to do—the "as far as it depends on you" bit—and leave the rest to the other person and to God.

Learn to forgive, relentlessly. Yes, there is pain and cost when we forgive someone. But although you let the person off your hook, they're not off God's hook. You can hand all of that pain, and those demands for justice and revenge, over to God, safe in the knowledge that justice will be done. In the meantime, you can walk free of it, and you can prevent Satan getting a foothold in your church fellowship.

I've got two left feet. But I love it when my kids want to dance with me. But just as it takes two to tango, it also takes two to cause division. So resolutely refuse to have any part in division.

As far as it depends on us, let's do everything we can to unleash the spiritual power that unity brings in the place where God has put us.

PAUSE FOR THOUGHT 1

OBJECTIVE

To consider further why the concept of "one body" is so important.

1. "Together we are God's chosen instrument to disciple the nations. There is no Plan B." Do you find this statement encouraging or daunting? Why?

2. Why, of all the things He could have prayed for those of us who would come after the first disciples, do you think that Jesus chose to pray that we would be one?

PART B

APPROACHING THOSE WHO DO NOT YET KNOW JESUS

Perhaps we've given you the impression that all we need to do is love each other, and people out there will flock into God's Kingdom. But, of course, we also need to go out and actually tell people about Jesus and work for justice and righteousness in our communities.

Our unity creates the necessary spiritual environment for those things to be much more fruitful.

So in this section, we want to consider how the God who is love calls us to approach people who don't yet know Jesus. We'll also think about how we approach *each other* when sin issues arise.

We saw in Session 3 how the Church became "judgey," and in many places came to see itself as responsible for the morals of the whole nation. Instead of astonishing people by our acts of love and showing that we are *for* them, we've become known for what we're *against*.

The problem is, you can't preach the good news but be the bad news.

But doesn't God want us to tell people what they're doing wrong?

Paul wrote a letter to the Corinthians in which he told them not to associate with sexually immoral people. And they totally misunderstood what he meant. He had to write them again to explain more fully, and here's what he said:

> I wrote to you in my letter not to associate with sexually immoral people—not at all meaning the people of this world who are immoral, or the greedy and swindlers, or idolaters. In that case you would have to leave this world. But now I am writing to you that you must not associate with anyone who claims to be a brother or sister but is sexually immoral or greedy, an idolater or slanderer, a drunkard or swindler. (1 Corinthians 5:9–11 NIV)

They had assumed that Paul meant they should not associate with sexually immoral people *outside* the Church. As if they were the weaker party and would somehow be contaminated by the world.

But Paul clearly says that when it comes to these sin issues, our concern should rather be those *inside* the Church who persistently sin. And let's notice that he doesn't just focus on those who commit sexual sins, but he puts equal weight on those who always want more things, or lash out with their tongues, or keep getting drunk.

In his letter to the Romans, Paul explains in graphic detail the dire situation that those who don't yet know Jesus are in: their thinking has become futile, their hearts are "darkened," and they indulge in impurity, unnatural sexual passions, murder, deceit, pride, and heartlessness. He affirms that "the judgment of God rightly falls on those who practice such things" (Romans 2:2).

He then gives a stern warning:

> Do you suppose, O man—you who judge those who practice such things and yet do them yourself—that you will escape the judgment of God? Or do you presume on the riches of his kindness and forbearance and patience, not knowing that God's kindness is meant to lead you to repentance? (Romans 2:2–4)

Surprisingly perhaps, this warning is not for the people out in the world who are actually caught in these things. It's for Christians who, despite having experienced God's grace, let their own standards slip—and yet feel free to condemn others.

The kindness of God that they had experienced was meant to lead them to repentance, not give them freedom to sin. And right there you have another counterintuitive characteristic of grace: it's *kindness,* not condemnation, that leads people to repentance.

But if we don't point out the sin in the world, doesn't that send a message that what they're doing is okay?

Well, that's not how Jesus worked. We don't see Him pointing out the sin of a tax collector, yet Zaccheus promised to repay everything he'd stolen. A prostitute made an extravagant public display of repentance, and Jesus hadn't even said a word.

God doesn't want us to *judge* people for their brokenness. He wants us to show them the way out of it. With kindness. So every single person should know they are welcome in our churches, no matter what kind of darkness they are living with or in. When they meet people who are experiencing freedom from the power of sin and the fear of death, they're surely going to want some of that, too!

We now have a church inside that prison in Uganda. Some of the guys who arrive are murderers and sex offenders. But we welcome them to our church. Many of them respond to this kindness with repentance. They turn to Jesus and experience His forgiveness and salvation.

APPROACHING THOSE WHO DO KNOW JESUS

Now once someone turns to Christ, we don't encourage them to continue living in ways that God warns against. We expect to see dramatic change. Jesus wants the actions of His Church to reflect the purity and holiness that He has given her.

So, do we line up these new Christians against a wall as soon as they believe in Jesus and say, "Now, you need to stop that . . . and that . . . and that!" No! We don't start by telling them what's *wrong* with them—we need to start by telling them what's *right* with them! What we *do* comes from who we *are*! They need to know that they are now holy, that they are loved, and that Jesus calls them to incredible fruitfulness.

They also need to know that, when God tells us not to do something, it's not because He's some kind of killjoy. It's because Jesus came specifically to set them free from slavery to sin.

When James discerned that some fellow Christians had a problem with the way they spoke, here's how he approached them. He said:

> Out of the same mouth, come praise and cursing. My brothers and sisters, this should not be. Can both fresh water and salt water flow from the same spring? My brothers and sisters, can a fig tree bear olives, or a grapevine bear figs? Neither can a salt spring produce fresh water. (James 3:10–12 NIV)

He doesn't use harsh words. He just makes the simple point that a fresh water spring doesn't produce salt water—it just doesn't. And in the same way, a fig tree doesn't bear olives—of course it doesn't. And when I lose my temper, grumble, or dwell on a lustful thought, I am acting out of character.

Deep down inside, we are now holy ones. And, if everything is working as it should, we'll do the things that holy ones do. It really is as simple as that.

If people refuse to respond to the gentle approach, on rare occasions church leaders will need to exercise discipline. Out of love. This is not about punishing people. Godly discipline is about helping them not to make the same mistake again. It's about restoration. It's kind.

I remember being on a leadership team once where one member misappropriated a large sum of money. They stole it. We could have punished them or expelled them. But they were genuinely repentant, and Galatians 6:1 says: "You who are spiritual should restore him in a spirit of gentleness." That's what we chose to do. Yes, there was discipline involved. But we told them what was right about them, and how what they had done was inconsistent with who they are, and how it would lead to bondage. And that person responded well and has gone from strength to strength, entering into greater and greater works that God has prepared for them.

It's kindness, not condemnation, that leads people to repentance!

PAUSE FOR THOUGHT 2

OBJECTIVE

To think through how God wants us to approach people outside the body of Christ and those inside.

1. How do you think it works that kindness leads people to repentance? Where have you seen this happening?

2. How can telling new Christians what is right with them (now that they are in Christ) help them become fruitful disciples?

3. How would you sum up the differences in the way we are called to approach those outside the body of Christ compared to those inside?

PART C

WHAT IS TRUE UNITY?

Paul tells us to be "eager to *maintain* the unity of the Spirit in the bond of peace" (Ephesians 4:3). And when I think that this is what enables us to exercise our spiritual authority to make disciples, I can certainly be eager about that!

That word *maintain* tells us we are already united at one level. But who exactly are we united with?

"If you declare with your mouth, 'Jesus is Lord,' and believe in your heart that God raised him from the dead, you will be saved" (Romans 10:9 NIV). Declare, believe. That's it. If any of you have done that, you're already united with each other in Christ—whether you like it or not! Are you going through this in a group? Look around the room—yes, united even with them!

And what does unity look like? Agreement on doctrine? When churches believed that, what was the outcome? Split after split after painful split.

We're not saying that good doctrine isn't important. It most definitely is. As we've seen, the Bible is the Word of God, and understanding what it says is crucial. The early church formulated statements of truth to help ensure people understood key elements. One of these early statements is 1 Corinthians 15:3–5. And it's fascinating that it lists just three key things:

- Christ died for our sins according to the Scriptures;

- He was buried;

- He was raised on the third day.

If someone doesn't believe these *essential* doctrines, it's difficult to imagine that they actually know Jesus at all. But just three things!

Now it's definitely good to seek out the truth of God's Word on other less essential matters. That's what we've been doing on this course. But as we've seen, although truth never changes, our *understanding* of truth can change.

However, the minute we insist that our current understanding of a nonessential doctrine is better than someone else's, we're no longer walking in love, but in pride. We are valuing a difference more than we value our relationship with our brothers and sisters in Christ.

100% GRACE AND 100% TRUTH

Jesus came to us "full of grace and truth" (John 1:14). 100 percent grace and 100 percent truth. Every generation faces big, seemingly intractable issues of doctrine that challenge our unity. Let's see how Paul addressed the big unity issue in the Church of his day with 100 percent grace and 100 percent truth.

He tells Gentile Christians (in 1 Corinthians 8) that it's perfectly okay to eat meat that's been offered to idols—that's the truth. But, then he follows it up with grace and tells them that if they do it in the presence of someone who believes, it's not okay, *then* it becomes sin.

The sin is not the eating of the meat, it's wounding the conscience of a brother or sister in Christ who has a different understanding of a nonessential question. The onus is on the person who thinks they have the correct doctrine—which, of course, we all do!—to act with grace toward those who believe something different.

As a new Christian I was a part of the praise and worship team of a small church—maybe not so much for my singing ability but possibly more for my passion for worship. We were invited to lead worship at a church which doesn't believe in women wearing make-up. I disagree with them. I was sorely tempted to show my "freedom" loud and clear by putting on my brightest lipstick! A wise lady on the team helped me see sense. And I chose to maintain the unity of the Spirit through the bond of peace. No lipstick. Today, one of my closest Christian friends is a beautiful young lady who holds some similar views. God has a sense of humor!

Are you excited about true unity and the spiritual power it releases? Are you up for being a peacemaker?

Unless you have really understood God's incredible grace, it's difficult to lay down the pride that makes us want to prove we're right; or the fear that makes us shy away from working with those from other parts of the body of Christ.

We've got two invitations for you as we come to a close.

First we want to invite you to commit to maintain the unity of the Spirit in the bond of peace. There's a prayer in your notes. If you are up for this, please join in as we pray it together:

Lord Jesus,

We join You in Your prayer to the Father that Your children would be one—because, like You, we want the world to believe that the Father sent You. You have said in Your Word that where there is unity You command a blessing, and we want to see that blessing come in full force. Just as You—the great King of kings—humbled Yourself by taking the form of a servant, even to the point of choosing to die a humiliating and agonizing death on a cross, we choose to give up our pretensions of being in any way righteous or right in our own strength, and we humble ourselves before You.

It's all about You and Your Kingdom, Lord, and not about us. We choose also to humble ourselves before each other in Christ and to come not just with truth but with grace— just as You come to us. We choose to consider others more important than ourselves and to put their interests above our own. We recognize that without genuine love, anything we do is no more than a noisy gong or clanging cymbal.

Even if our Christian doctrine and tradition are 100 percent right, without love they are worth nothing.

Lord, we are eager to maintain the unity of the Spirit in the bond of peace. We therefore ask You to fill us afresh with the Holy Spirit and to lead us in love.

We choose to be peacemakers, not nitpickers.

We choose relationship above rules.

We choose love above law.

We choose to be real rather than right.

We pray all this in the Name of the humble Jesus, the One who has now been lifted up to the very highest place and who has the Name that is above every other name, Amen.

This is the last of our main teaching sessions but we look forward to seeing you again for *The Steps To Experiencing God's Grace*. It's a kind, gentle process where you ask the Holy Spirit to show you any issues He wants you to work on and deal with.

We'll then show you how you can go on to replace any lies you've believed with the truth from God's Word using "Stronghold-Busting." And that's what will make this course not just something nice you did for eight weeks, but something that has an ongoing transformational effect in your life. You won't want to miss it!

THE WEDDING CELEBRATION

Now, we mentioned *two* invitations. The second is a wedding invitation. Revelation 7:9 tells us that, at the end of time, "A great multitude that no one could number, from every nation, from all tribes and peoples and languages" will assemble, and there will be a wedding to end all weddings.

And because we know Jesus, we're invited! I used to think, "I'm pretty sure I'll make it onto the guest list, but

I'll probably be at the back where the groom seats the questionable friends that he doesn't really want his new mother-in-law to meet. . . ."

It only recently hit me that we're not *guests* at this wedding! We are the *bride*! We're right there, top table, with the groom.

And we—the Church—will be married to Jesus, the Lamb of God.

As *individual* Christians, we stand with our sandals, our ring, and our robe. But *together* as the Bride of Christ, we, the Church, will be unimaginably glorious.

And God has such confidence in us that in Revelation 19:7, we see in black and white that we, His bride, *will* have made ourselves ready.

And that is definitely something I can be both passionate and eager about, and work towards for the rest of my life—in His power and by His grace.

REFLECT

Introduction

How you can play your part in preparing the Bride of Christ for His glorious return.

Reflection

Invite the Holy Spirit to show you any times where you have been arrogant toward other Christians.

Read John 3:17 and then ask the Holy Spirit to show you any times when you have condemned those who do not yet know Jesus.

How can you play your part in helping the Bride prepare herself for Jesus' return?

We invite you to finish this time by speaking out the Prayer for Unity below.

> CONCLUDING THE SESSION

Now that we are coming to the end of the course, let people know about *The Wonder Of Grace* by Rich Miller, a book that has been written specifically to help participants of *The Grace Course* take the principles taught deeper. It consists of forty days of readings that explore just what it means to live a grace-filled life.

It's now time for participants to go through *The Steps To Experiencing God's Grace*. Emphasize the importance of this, and run through the arrangements.

Close in prayer.

PRAYER FOR UNITY

Lord Jesus,

We join You in Your prayer to the Father that Your children would be one—because, like You, we want the world to believe that the Father sent You. You have said in Your Word that where there is unity You command a blessing, and we want to see that blessing come in full force. Just as You—the great King of kings—humbled Yourself by taking the form of a servant, even to the point of choosing to die a humiliating and agonizing death on a cross, we choose to give up our pretensions of being in any way righteous or right in our own strength and we humble ourselves before You.

It's all about You and Your Kingdom, Lord, and not about us. We choose also to humble ourselves before each other in Christ and to come not just with truth but with grace—just as You come to us. We choose to consider others more important than ourselves and to put their interests above our own. We recognize that without genuine love, anything we do is no more than a noisy gong or clanging cymbal.

Even if our Christian doctrine and tradition are 100 percent right, without love they are worth nothing.

Lord, we are eager to maintain the unity of the Spirit in the bond of peace. We therefore ask You to fill us afresh with the Holy Spirit and to lead us in love.

We choose to be peacemakers, not nitpickers.

We choose relationship above rules.

We choose love above law.

We choose to be real rather than right.

We pray all this in the Name of the humble Jesus, the One who has now been lifted up to the very highest place and who has the Name that is above every other name, Amen.

(Based on Psalm 133, John 1:14–17, John 17:20–23, 1 Corinthians 13, Ephesians 4:1–7, Philippians 2:1–11)

THE STEPS TO EXPERIENCING GOD'S GRACE

OBJECTIVE

To ask the Holy Spirit to reveal areas where we need to repent so that we can resolve personal and spiritual conflicts, remove "false motivators," and go on to a live out of a deep appreciation of God's grace.

FOCUS VERSE

Submit yourselves therefore to God. Resist the devil, and he will flee from you.

James 4:7

 **FOCUS TRUTH**

Christ has set us free (Galatians 5:1), but we will not experience that freedom without genuine repentance.

 **CONNECT**

Confession (admitting that we did wrong) is the first step to repentance but is not enough on its own. We must both submit to God and resist the devil. We must also make a choice about what we believe and how we are living and decide to change. If we want to grow in Christ, we must choose to renounce the lies we have believed and any sin in our lives, and announce our choice to believe that what God says is true and start to live accordingly.

LEADER'S NOTES

The notes for this session are different from others in the course because for the most part they are intended primarily for the leader of the session rather than being a script. We recommend that you read through the notes and instructions for the session thoroughly before leading it and also view *The Steps To Experiencing God's Grace* session on video if possible.

There are two ways to lead this session. You can either use *The Steps To Experiencing God's Grace* session on video (available separately—see page 19) or lead it yourself using the notes that follow. Each participant will need their own copy of *The Steps To Experiencing God's Grace* which is in their Participant's Guide or online notes.

You will also need a copy, as the process itself is not printed in this Leader's Guide.

We recommend that everyone who does *The Grace Course* goes through *The Steps To Freedom In Christ* before going through *The Steps To Experiencing God's Grace* if possible.

The process is straightforward: the participants ask the Holy Spirit to show them areas in their lives where they need to repent, and then choose to do so. We would encourage you to go through the process yourself before leading others through. Being able to share your own experiences of going through the process with your group gives them the assurance that they are not being asked to do something you haven't first done yourself.

A suggested timetable for an Away Day retreat is on page 171.

> INTRODUCTION

Seeing people go through *The Steps To Experiencing God's Grace* is exciting! It's a gentle, kind, undramatic process, but it can make an enormous difference to their lives. There is no need to feel nervous about leading the process. You are simply facilitating an encounter between those seeking freedom and Jesus who is the Wonderful Counselor.

The Steps To Experiencing God's Grace has the following benefits:

- The method is transferable because it doesn't require experts—it can be conducted by any reasonably mature Christian who is walking in freedom.

- It produces lasting results because the "freedom-seekers" are the ones making the decisions and assuming personal responsibility, rather than a pastor or counselor doing it for them.

- It doesn't bypass the person's mind.

- The focus is on Christ and repentance. The real issue isn't Satan; it is God and our walk with Him.

- The seven steps cover seven issues that are critical between ourselves and God.

The Steps To Experiencing God's Grace doesn't set anyone free! *Who* sets them free is Christ. *What* sets them free is their response to Him in repentance and faith.

> APPROACHES TO TAKING PEOPLE THROUGH THE STEPS

Participants should be given an opportunity to go through *The Steps To Experiencing God's Grace* at the end of *The Grace Course* as soon as possible after Session 8. The *Stronghold-Busting* session should be run after the *Steps*, either by combining it with the *Steps* session or in a separate session soon afterward.

There are two different ways you can approach the *Steps,* and you need to decide well in advance of starting the course which will suit your situation:

1. AN INDIVIDUAL GRACE STEPS APPOINTMENT

This is the ideal. In this scenario each individual is led through the process by an "encourager," with a prayer partner in attendance, in a session that typically lasts three or four hours. It can be incredibly uplifting when people in a church or small group are willing to confess their sins to one another and pray for each other (see James 5:16). Encouragers and prayer partners do not generally need any special skills other than a reasonable maturity in Christ and an understanding of the Biblical principles of freedom, but will benefit from having attended a *Helping Others Find Freedom In Christ* course or having read *Discipleship Counseling* by Neil Anderson (Regal Books, 2003).

2. AS A GROUP ON AN AWAY DAY RETREAT

Taking your group away for a day (or even a weekend) to go through the *Steps* works well. It allows everyone to go through the *Steps* at the same time whilst ensuring that people have enough time to do business with any issues that the Holy Spirit brings to their mind. It is best to book a location away from your church and to include times of worship. You will need leaders to make themselves available to participants who may need help at various times. Whether or not your group has already been through *The Freedom In Christ Course*, it can be helpful to include Session 7—*Forgiving From The Heart* from that course in the Away Day retreat directly before your group goes through *Step Four: Forgiving Others.*

Even if you are using the Away Day retreat approach, you will need to make some provision for personal appointments. We recommend that those leading the course have personal appointments, for example, and you will probably find that people with deeper issues will not be able to get everything done on the away day retreat, or, will struggle, and will need a personal appointment. Simply see how they get on and arrange a personal appointment afterward if needed.

Some churches have successfully run *the Steps* online, both as individual appointments and as an Away Day retreat.

> TAKING AN INDIVIDUAL THROUGH THE STEPS TO EXPERIENCING GOD'S GRACE

1. PREPARATION

The person going through the process (the "freedom-seeker") should have completed a Confidential Personal Inventory before the appointment. Registered users of *The Grace Course* can download a sample document and you have permission to copy this and adapt it for your own use. Bear in mind, however, that many people will not disclose certain confidential information in writing so there may well be more to come out. The Confidential Personal Inventory provides important information concerning their physical, mental, emotional and spiritual life. However, its primary function is to help the freedom-seeker prepare for their appointment. You should return it to them at the end of the appointment.

Choose a comfortable room and allow for several hours. Have a box of tissues available and some water. Take occasional breaks. We strongly recommend that you get the freedom-seeker to complete a Statement of Understanding which confirms for legal reasons their understanding that the encourager is not functioning as a trained counselor. It contains no personal information beyond the name of the person and date of the appointment and should be filed in your records. There is a sample Statement of Understanding to download that you may adapt for your own use.

2. LEAD THEM THROUGH THE STEPS TO EXPERIENCING GOD'S GRACE

The primary focus of the *Steps* for the freedom-seeker is their own relationship with God. The process is different from most counseling approaches, because the one who is praying is the one who needs the help, and they are praying to the only One who can help them.

It is recommended that as well as the leader ("the encourager") and the freedom-seeker, a prayer partner is also present.

Explain to the freedom-seeker what they are doing and why they are doing it. Try to go through all seven steps in one session. They may not need every step but you want to be thorough for their sake. Have them read every prayer and affirmation out loud. Ask them to share with you any mental opposition or physical discomfort. When they do, thank them for sharing it with you. Once it is acknowledged, simply go on. In most cases there is very little opposition.

Step Four: Forgiving Others is usually the most critical step. Every person has at least one person and usually several people to forgive. Unforgiveness affords the biggest door into the Church for Satan. If we can't help a person forgive from the heart, we can't help them be free from their past. When they pray and ask God whom they need to forgive, rest assured that God does reveal names to their mind. If they say, "Well there is no one," then respond by saying, "Would you just share the names that are coming to your mind right now?" Usually, several names will surface, and they should record them on a sheet of paper. It is not uncommon for freedom-seekers to have names come to mind that surprise them. And it is not uncommon for them to recall forgotten painful memories while in the process of forgiving.

Explain what forgiveness is and how to do it. There is a brief summary in the Participant's Guide. Once they have completed their list of names ask if they would be willing to forgive those people for their own sake. Forgiving others is primarily an issue between them and their Heavenly Father. Reconciliation may or may not follow.

3. KEEP POINTING THEM TOWARD TRUTH

Getting free in Christ is one thing; staying free is another. Paul says in Galatians 5:1 (NASB), "It was for freedom that Christ set you free; therefore keep standing firm and do not be subject again to a yoke of slavery."

Talk to them about the key things that have been raised during the appointment to help them uncover lies. Most people caught in a spiritual conflict have a distorted concept of God and themselves, and it will help you if you can determine what those false beliefs are. Defeated Christians often have a distorted concept of the two kingdoms. They think they are caught between two equal but opposite powers. Bad old Satan is on one side, good old God is on the other, and poor old me is caught in the middle. That of course is not true, and they are defeated if that is what they believe. The truth is God is omnipresent, omnipotent, and omniscient. Satan is a defeated foe, and we are alive in Christ, and seated with Him at the right hand of the Father, the ultimate seat of power and authority in the universe.

The *Stronghold-Busting* session will show them how to replace lies they have identified with truth so that they can renew their minds, which is what will bring genuine transformation (see Romans 12:2).

The freedom-seeker will derive enormous benefit if you can keep encouraging them to: identify lies, list Bible verses that say what is really true, develop Stronghold-Busters and persevere through them (one at a time) for forty days.

> TAKING A GROUP THROUGH *THE STEPS TO EXPERIENCING GOD'S GRACE* ON AN AWAY DAY RETREAT

You will find a suggested timetable for an Away Day retreat on page 171 to assist in planning. You will find it very helpful to watch the video beforehand.

It is recommended that you hold the Away Day retreat in pleasant surroundings, away from your church if possible. Aim to provide lunch, or make sure that people bring packed lunches—it is recommended that you maintain a quiet atmosphere over lunchtime and suggest that people remain on the premises.

The room you use should be large enough for participants to have some degree of privacy. It is helpful if people can spread out. Have some quiet music playing in the background so that people can pray out loud without feeling that others are listening. Instrumental music works best as it is less distracting.

Each participant will need their Participant's Guide, which contains *The Steps To Experiencing God's Grace*. A means to take notes is also helpful.

Most use the video of the *Steps* session to guide people through the process because it does most of the work for you. You will obviously need appropriate technology so that everyone can see it.

People will at times benefit from individual attention during those steps that they find difficult. Plan to have a reasonable number of people whose role is to walk around and help those who are struggling (one for every ten people would be a good starting point). These should be mature Christians who have been through the *Steps* themselves.

Start with prayer, and then explain how the session will work. The group will be praying several prayers together out loud. Then they will spend some time alone with God. Nobody will be embarrassed or asked to share anything with the group or another person. It is solely an encounter with God.

Explain to the group that some will get in touch with real pain, and tears are understandable and acceptable. Some people will have very little to deal with on some steps, whereas others may have a lot. You can suggest that those who do not have much on a particular step spend time praying for those who do, that the Holy Spirit will reveal everything that needs to be revealed, and that Satan's attempts to interfere in the process will be ineffective. If people have too much to deal with in the time available, reassure them that this is not a one-off opportunity and that they will be able to catch up in due course, ideally by having their own personal appointment.

Start each step with a brief explanation of what it is about, get everyone to say the opening prayers together, and then allow them time alone with God to deal with the issues the Holy Spirit shows them. Wait until everybody has finished that step or that part of the step and is ready to continue before moving on to the next video.

The following notes are to guide you, especially if you are leading without the video. They are written from the point of view of a group leader speaking to their group, and are meant to prompt you as you introduce each part of the process.

Explain the steps and then have the group pray together and out loud the prayer that begins each step. Then allow them to have time alone with God.

NOTES FOR THE GROUP LEADER

[For each step these notes contain an introduction and then a bullet-pointed list of things that need to be done.]

INTRODUCTION

Welcome to *The Steps To Experiencing God's Grace*, a kind and gentle way to help you ensure that the Biblical principles we've looked at in *The Grace Course* become real in your experience.

Do you want to grow in Christ, learn to live the "grace-rest" life, and bear fruit that will last for eternity? Then you're in the right place!

Do you feel distant from God? Has your Christian walk become a bit heavy or feel a burden? Are you struggling to break free from slavery to sin or fear? You are going to have the opportunity to allow God to gently and lovingly to show you the way forward and begin again.

Remember, God is love. And He loves *you*! There is now no condemnation from Him. Now means now. And no means no!

All He wants to do is open your eyes as gently as possible to areas where you are struggling. He doesn't want you to feel guilt or shame or fear. In fact, He wants you to be free from these things so you can experience His love at an even deeper level.

I suspect that God is excited about the prospect that at the end of this session you may experience an intimacy and closeness to Him that perhaps you have not felt in a while—or perhaps ever. There is nothing to fear, only good things to look forward to.

You will need a copy of *The Grace Course Participant's Guide* which contains the prayers, declarations, and notes we'll go through, or access to that material online.

I would encourage you to spread out in the room, putting some space between yourself and the person next to you—even if that person is your spouse. You can get close again later on! But the idea is that as you go through the Steps, this is a personal encounter with the Living God and you want to minimize any possible distractions to that time with Him.

For each Step, we will first of all give you some basic information about the Step and its purpose. Then we'll take you through the process of actually going through the Step, including an opening prayer that we will pray out loud together. The prayers and declarations are all labeled with a number and a letter to help you locate them.

Next you will be free to work by yourself to see what the Holy Spirit brings to your mind in that Step, dealing with whatever He shows you.

In these personal, private prayer times with God, I suggest that you pray out loud, maybe in a soft whisper or low mutter so that others can't hear. That accomplishes at least three things. First, it helps you concentrate because it's much easier to get distracted when you are praying silent prayers in your mind. Second, it will help reinforce what you're doing as you remember much more of what you say and hear as opposed to what you just think. And third, it will serve notice to the enemy that you mean business because he can hear what you say out loud but isn't aware of all that you think to yourself.

Moving from a place of shame, guilt, fear, anxiety, or pride can meet with some resistance from our enemy. Usually it comes in the form of thoughts in your mind about this being a waste of time or too hard or that you need to leave the session to do something else. Just stand firm and ask God to give you the strength to persevere through, and you'll be so glad you did.

If you find yourself really struggling with annoying thoughts, tell the enemy to "take a hike in the name of Jesus" and continue on. You can also ask one of the leaders of the session to pray with you. But remember, Jesus has already disarmed all the powers of darkness, and He shares His authority with you to send the enemy on his way. James 4:7 assures us that, as you submit to God and resist the devil, he has no option but to flee from you.

There are two main things that will happen during this process.

First, the Holy Spirit will help you see areas of sin that are giving the enemy some influence in your life. As you submit to God by acknowledging the issues and turning away from them, you will close the "doors" you opened. And at the end of the process you will resist the devil. And he will have no option but to flee from you.

The second thing that will happen is that the Holy Spirit will enable you to see areas where your beliefs have been out of line with what is actually true according to God's Word, the Bible. It's replacing those lies with truth—what the Bible calls "renewing your mind"—that will bring lasting transformation. After you've been through these Steps, we'll equip you with a tool called "Stronghold-Busting" that you can use for the rest of your life to do just that, whenever you become aware that your belief system is out of kilter with the Bible.

You will find it really helpful to take a sheet of paper or find a place in your phone to record the faulty beliefs that come to mind during the Steps. Just write them down in a Lies List, and you can address them with Stronghold-Busting.

OPENING PRAYER AND DECLARATION

Before beginning these Steps, you may find it helpful to look at the introduction in the Participant's Guide.

There are a number of prayers and declarations that we'll invite you to speak out loud with us. All of them are labeled at the bottom with a number and a letter so that you can identify which one to go to. What's the difference between a prayer and a declaration? Well, a prayer is spoken to God. And a declaration is spoken to all in the spiritual world: God, angels, demons.

We're going to start with the Opening Prayer which is prayer 1.A. And follow that immediately with the Opening Declaration, 1.B.

STEP ONE: CHOOSING TO BELIEVE THE TRUTH

In this first Step, we will affirm some key truths from the Bible. Jesus told us that knowing the truth sets us free. So, by implication, believing lies keeps us in bondage. It is important to reject all the lies you have become aware of during *The Grace Course* and instead choose to declare and believe what is actually true according to God's Word. God may also use the affirmations to reveal more faulty thinking to you.

For example, if a true follower of Christ knows that he or she is totally forgiven, completely accepted, unconditionally loved, and absolutely safe and secure in Christ, would those truths positively impact that person's life? Of course! In the same way, if that same person were instead haunted by guilt and shame, unsure of God's love, plagued with unhealthy fears, or swelled up with pride, would believing the lies associated with those problems negatively affect his or her life? Of course they would!

So in order to be a healthy, growing, fruitful disciple of Jesus, we need to know, believe, and live in accordance with the truth and reject any lies we realize we've been believing about who we are in Christ and about God's nature and attitude toward us.

Pray Prayer 1.C aloud together.

Having a wrong view of God's character and His expectations of us will really get in the way of a close, intimate relationship with Him. So we're going to start by considering the truth about our Father God that we looked at in Session 6 of *The Grace Course*.

We will reject out loud common lies that Christians often believe about God and affirm what is actually true from the Bible.

Say Declaration 1.D out loud together.

Now take some time alone with God to look back over the list and mark any truths that are difficult for you to receive in your heart. You may like to look up the Bible references of those particular truths. Then when you are ready, for each one you've marked, use Prayer 1.E on your own to affirm what is true about God. Where there is a blank space, use your own words or what is written in the second half of the statements in the declaration. Record any lies about God you have believed in your Lies List.

Pause

STEP TWO: WALKING BY THE SPIRIT RATHER THAN THE FLESH

There's a huge contrast between the two brothers in Jesus' story of the prodigal. The younger son lived under the delusion that "the good life" was out there somewhere away from any structure or restraints, rules or expectations that his father or anyone else might have. But he discovered that freedom wasn't found "out there" living the wild life.

Even though we are now new creations in Christ at the deepest level of our beings, we still have a tendency toward sin that the Bible calls "the flesh." Every day we can choose either to walk by the Spirit or by the flesh. In this Step, we'll invite our Father to show us where we have believed the lies that the flesh feeds us and allowed ourselves to return to slavery to sin.

Confession literally means "to say the same thing" or come into agreement with someone. When we confess our sins to God, we are saying that He is right in His assessment that what we've done is wrong. We admit He is right and we were wrong. And let's also remember to come into agreement with what He tells us in 1 John 1:9: "If we confess our sins, he is faithful and righteous to forgive us our sins and to cleanse us from all unrighteousness."

Forgiveness takes care of the guilt of our sins; cleansing takes care of the shame.

We can come to God humbly and freely and acknowledge our wrongdoing because God is gracious and merciful, slow to anger and compassionate. He knows all about our sin, yet that doesn't change His love for us even a bit. Remember, "there is therefore now no condemnation for those who are in Christ Jesus" (Romans 8:1).

Say Prayer 2.A aloud together.

Take a look at the list of sins of the flesh in your notes. They are based on Galatians 5:19–21 but of course there are others. Take your time and allow the Holy Spirit to show you which you need to deal with today. Then mark those or write them in.

Finally, on your own, use Prayer 2.B to confess them and turn away from them. Take your time to do this thoroughly.

Pause

STEP THREE: PRIDE, PERFORMANCE, AND PERFECTIONISM

In this Step, we will consider the errors that the elder brother fell into. He mistakenly believed that he had to earn anything that would come from his father. He slaved away in joyless labor, strangled by the structure, restraints, and rules he allowed to control him. But all along he could have been enjoying everything the father had.

We're going to begin this Step by asking God to reveal to us the expectations, standards, and demands of others that we have felt we need to live up to in order to feel good about ourselves, to measure up, or to be acceptable.

Pray Prayer 3.A out loud together.

Now spend time evaluating where you've lived under false expectations and write the false expectations, standards, and demands you have lived under on a separate sheet of paper or on your phone. Then use Prayer 3.B to reject them. You may then like to rip up the false expectations you wrote down or delete them with a particular flourish to emphasize that they are now gone!

Pause

Maybe you've struggled to please people and you have a hard time saying no. Maybe you've lived under a yoke of perfectionism trying to live up to your own expectations. Perhaps you've even envisaged God as a harsh, cruel

taskmaster who is rarely pleased, seldom smiling, and never satisfied with what you do. Or you realize that you have acted out of pride. Remember that God opposes the proud and that humility is the key to unity and answering Jesus' prayer in John 17 that we would be one.

Pray Prayer 3.C out loud together.

Take your time as you consider potential areas of weakness in the areas of performance, perfectionism, pride and judgmentalism, power and control, and pleasureless living. Let the Holy Spirit point out to you actions and attitudes that you need to deal with and mark them.

Then use Prayer 3.D to confess them and turn away from them, remembering to add lies you realize you've been believing to your Lies List.

Pause

STEP FOUR: FORGIVING OTHERS

Consider showing the video from Session 7, *Forgiving From The Heart,* of *The Freedom In Christ Course,* as an introduction to this Step. This is included at no additional cost if you are accessing the video via Freedom In Christ's Discipleship Hub.

One of the things that is an obvious difference between the father and the elder son in Jesus' story of the prodigal is that the father forgave his younger son but the elder brother did not. The father was filled with joy but the elder brother was filled with anger and resentment.

Holding on to unforgiveness doesn't hurt the person who hurt you. It hurts *you*. And God invites you to hand them and what they did over to Him in the sure knowledge that He is the righteous judge and He will make it right in the end (Romans 12:19).

This may be the most liberating step for you as you allow God to show you the people that have hurt you, pressured you to conform, abused you physically, verbally, emotionally, or sexually, or in some other way tried to control you.

Pray Prayer 4.A out loud together.

Now take some time simply to write down the names the Holy Spirit brings to your mind.

Pause

Did you consider forgiving yourself? You may have believed the lie that you deserve to be beaten up for what you did, so you beat yourself up. But consider this: Jesus was beaten up—more than that, He suffered and died—so that you would not have to be. His death is the full payment for sins—yours and mine. On the cross He cried out, "It is finished!" and He meant it. Experiencing God's forgiveness in your own life frees you to forgive others. So, add yourself to the list now if you need to.

And did you think about forgiving God Himself? Of course, God hasn't done anything wrong. But if we are to forgive from the heart, we need to be honest about how we feel. He has never left us or abandoned us—but we may have felt that He did. It can be really helpful to express that we forgive Him, which really means that we're making a decision to acknowledge and release the negative thoughts we've had about Him. He's plenty big enough to take it. He won't be offended. In fact, He'll just delight in the freedom this will bring you.

When we forgive, we are most like Christ. All God is asking us to do is to place our relationship with those who have hurt us on the same basis as God has placed His relationship with us.

When we forgive, we give someone a gift they don't deserve. We cancel their debt and choose not to hold their sin against them any more.

Jesus makes it clear that our forgiveness must be sincere. We need to be real and honest with God about how we've been hurt and the cost to us personally. Then we can make the choice to cancel that debt because we are fully aware of the cost to us. So don't try and bypass your emotions by saying something really generic like, "Okay, I'll forgive that person." Get honest and get specific in your forgiveness like, "I choose to forgive my dad for beating me time and time again when I was little, even though I was only trying to do my best. I hated him for that and wished at times he would just leave us. I am still angry with him to this day. But I choose to give him the gift of forgiveness, and I release him into Your hands, God, and I give up any right to retain my resentment or lash out at him in revenge."

Is it easy? No. When we've been hurt badly, this is really hard. But how do you stop the pain? Certainly not by hanging on to the hurt and nursing the grudge. The only way to stop the pain and to move on into fruitfulness is to make the choice to forgive. We can't turn the clock back and change the past, but, through forgiving from the heart, we can be free from the past.

In God's strength, forgiving others *is* possible. He will give you the grace to forgive when you make the choice to do so. And it is a choice you *can* make because Christ lives in you.

Take a look at Prayers 4.B, 4.C, and 4.D. For each person on your list, pray Prayer 4.B. Forgive from the heart. Be totally honest with God. Take your time. If you feel able, write down what you say after the "which made me feel" part in Prayer 4.B. If you find the same word or expression repeated two or three times, it may indicate a false belief that you can deal with later using Stronghold-Busting.

Once you've finished, use Prayer 4.C to bless them.

Finally, use Prayer 4.D if you know you need to release God from negative thoughts you have held against Him.

Pause

STEP FIVE: FREEDOM FROM FEAR

In this Step, you will have the opportunity to identify and renounce any unhealthy, controlling fears. As we have seen in *The Grace Course* (in Session 5: *Courageous!*), not all fear is bad. Some fear makes all the sense in the world. You don't jump over the fence at the zoo to pet the nice big kitty, for example. But unhealthy fears hold us back from being the free, growing, and fruitful followers of Christ that God wants us to be. Those fears need to be renounced, and we need to choose to walk by faith in God instead.

In the first part of this Step we'll identify three things: **unhealthy fears** that are controlling us; the **lies** that fuel that fear; and the antidote, which is **the truth from God's Word**.

Every unhealthy, controlling fear is based on a lie. Usually it will have something to do with an inadequate grasp of who God is or who we are in Christ. Or believing that the object of your fear is both powerful and present when only one of those things is actually true. Whatever the lie may be, putting your finger on it, and being able to state it clearly, exposes the fear for what it is: a fraud!

Pray Prayer 5.A out loud together.

Now take a look at the list underneath prayer 5.A. This may help you recognize some of the unhealthy fears that are hindering your walk of faith. Mark the ones that apply to you and write them down together with any others that the Holy Spirit has revealed to you.

Write them in the first column of the table in your notes, or use a separate piece of paper—landscape format is best because you need to divide it into three columns and label them "Fear," "Lie," and "Truth."

For each of the fears, ask God to help you work out the lie behind it and then find the corresponding truth from His Word. There's an example in your notes. It may help to get some wisdom from a friend or a leader. Don't worry if you can't do all of it in the time available. Just come back later. But do ensure you complete the exercise.

Use Prayer 5.B to turn away from each fear, reject the lie behind it, and embrace the truth from God's Word.

Pause

The second part of this Step deals with the fear of people. Proverbs 29:25 (NIV) says, "Fear of man will prove to be a snare, but whoever trusts in the LORD is kept safe."

Fearing people ultimately leads to pleasing people. People-pleasers find themselves more and more concerned about what other people think because they wrongly believe that their personal worth and happiness are dependent upon the acceptance and approval of others.

So many times we allow peer pressure or the desire to fit in to keep us from living out the bold, confident, free life in Christ that brings us the deepest joy and the greatest glory to God. Renouncing those fears in this Step can be the beginning point of a change in your life that will dramatically increase the impact for Christ you make in this world.

Pray Prayer 5.C out loud together.

Consider the prompt list and put a mark beside any areas the Holy Spirit reveals to you. Then use Prayer 5.D to deal with them.

Pause

STEP SIX: EXCHANGING ANXIETY FOR GOD'S PEACE

Paul said, "Do not be anxious about anything, but in everything by prayer and supplication with thanksgiving let your requests be made known to God" (Philippians 4:6). Peter also told us to cast our anxiety onto Christ who cares for us (1 Peter 5:7). In this Step, we'll put into practice the principles we learned about casting our anxiety onto Christ in Session 6 of *The Grace Course*.

Prayer is the first step in casting all your anxiety on Christ. So let's pray.

Pray Prayer 6.A out loud together.

In your notes, you'll see a table with four columns based on the principles we taught in Session 6.

In the first column, list the situations that are causing you anxiety. But when you list them, ensure you step back from the situation and state the issue calmly and dispassionately.

Then focus on the facts of the situation and write them down in the second column.

It might also be helpful to list in the third column any assumptions you realize you've been making so that you can separate them from the facts and disregard them. It's amazing how easily our minds leap to the worst possible outcome, and, before we know it, we've convinced ourselves that that's what's going to happen! We need to stick to the facts of the situation.

Finally, work out prayerfully before God in the situation that is causing you anxiety:

- What is your responsibility?
- What is God's responsibility?
- And what is someone else's responsibility?

Record your own responsibilities in the fourth column. You might need to forgive someone. You might need to put something right.

The key principle here is that you can be responsible only for things that you have both the right and ability to control. You are not responsible when you don't.

The rest is God's responsibility.

Your only remaining responsibility is to continue to pray and focus on the truth according to Philippians 4:6–8. If you still feel anxious, check again that you aren't assuming responsibilities that God never intended you to have.

Use Prayer 6.B to assume your responsibilities once you have completed the four columns.

Pause

You probably have some responsibilities to assume that translate into things you actually need to do. Please don't forget to do them. Don't just pray about them—you can cast your anxieties on to Christ, but if you try casting your responsibilities on to Him, He will cast them right back at you!

But once you have fulfilled your responsibility, you can confidently say, "Over to you, God," and leave everything else with Him. Because He is real. He is strong. And He really does care about you.

You'll see in your notes an exercise you can do in the coming days to combat anxiety. There are also some practical suggestions in the notes for Session 6 of *The Grace Course*.

STEP SEVEN: SURRENDERING AS A LIVING SACRIFICE

The apostle Paul wrote in Romans 12:1, "Therefore, I urge you, brothers and sisters, in view of God's mercy, to offer your bodies as a living sacrifice, holy and pleasing to God—this is your true and proper worship" (NIV).

God wants us all to come to the place of surrender, where there is no part of our lives that we are consciously holding back from Him. Paul indicates that this is the spiritual and reasonable way to worship God because He is so kind and merciful to us.

Who would want to surrender to a mean and cruel God? No one! But to such a good, caring, loving, powerful, protecting God? How could we not give everything we are and everything we have and everything we hope for to Him for His safekeeping?

In this final Step, we list many different aspects of life that you may never have considered giving over to Him. Take your time. It requires weighty decisions to relinquish control of every area of life one by one. This must be your choice, of your own free will.

We believe you will be filled with great reassurance and peace when you give these things to God, but you'll have to wrestle through to that point yourself. It really does help to think about all the ways He has been so merciful to you.

Are you ready to make a commitment to God to love Him with an undivided heart, not because you are in any way compelled to, but simply out of love? It may feel scary but, in fact, when we surrender ourselves fully into the hands of our loving Father, we are putting ourselves in the only place where we are completely and utterly secure.

Let's ask God to show us the areas we need to surrender to Him.

Pray Prayer 7.A out loud together.

Take a look at the prompt list and mark any area you need to surrender to God. Then use Prayer 7.B to do that.

Pause

In the final prayer of surrender, we invite you to do three things:

First, to offer your whole self—all you are and all you have—to God as a living and holy sacrifice.

Second, to complete the process of submitting to God and resisting the devil by commanding every evil spirit to leave your presence.

And finally, now that God has emptied you of false beliefs and independent ways of living, ask Him to fill you afresh with His wonderful Holy Spirit, empowering you to live according to the law of the Spirit of life and freedom!

Pray Prayer 7.C out loud together.

Let's finish these Steps by affirming some of the great truths that we have considered on *The Grace Course*.

Say the Final Affirmations 7.D out loud together.

Now close your eyes for a minute and just be quiet.

In your mind, is it quiet? Is there a sense of peace?

You might feel on cloud nine right now, or you might just feel tired! Remember that the point of this process was not to get a good feeling. It was to deal with areas where you were being held back from being a fruitful disciple of

Jesus. If you have honestly dealt with everything the Holy Spirit has shown you today, then you can move forward, confident that the God of grace has amazing plans for you.

We haven't finished just yet. We've saved one of our most exciting and effective tools for discipleship until last.

You see, it's one thing to identify lies you've believed, and I hope you've managed to do that and that you have your Lies List handy. But it's another thing entirely to tear down those strongholds and replace them with truth.

Stronghold-Busting is a highly effective process that you can use to do that. And we will look at that in a final session of *The Grace Course*.

> CONCLUDING THE SESSION

Remind participants about *The Wonder Of Grace* by Rich Miller, a book that has been written specifically to help participants on *The Grace Course* take the principles taught deeper. It consists of forty days of readings that explore just what it means to live a grace-filled life.

Emphasize the importance of Stronghold-Busting for lasting transformation.

Close in prayer.

> SUGGESTED TIMETABLE FOR AN AWAY DAY RETREAT

This is a suggested timetable for taking a group through *The Steps To Experiencing God's Grace* on an away day retreat.

9.45   Welcome and worship (25 minutes)

10.10   Introduction/prayer/declaration (15 minutes)

10.25   Step 1: Choosing to Believe the Truth (30 minutes)

10:55   Step 2: Walking by the Spirit Rather than the Flesh (20 minutes)

11.15   Break (30 minutes)

11:45   Step 3: Pride, Performance, and Perfectionism (40 minutes)

12.25   Lunch Break

13.25   Video teaching on forgiveness from *The Freedom In Christ Course* (Session 7 - 40 minutes)

14.05   Step 4: Forgiveness (50 minutes)

14:55   Break (30 minutes)

15:25   Step 5: Freedom from Fear (30 minutes)

15:55   Step 6: Exchanging Anxiety for God's Peace (30 minutes)

16:25   Break if needed (15 minutes)

16:40   Step 7: Surrendering as a Living Sacrifice (15 minutes)

16.55   Worship and finish

This includes the video teaching on forgiveness from *The Freedom In Christ Course* (40 minutes) but you may decide not to do that.

It does not include the Stronghold-Busting session. Our recommendation is that, because this is so important to ongoing freedom and growth, you run it as a session in its own right in the following days. However, one option would be to insert it after Step 7, in which case you would need to add 20 minutes for the video teaching (not including the Pause For Thought) and 20 to 30 minutes for people to work on their first Stronghold-Buster.

Registered users of the course can download an Excel spreadsheet with these timings. Simply enter your own start time, adjust the length of the various components if desired, and you will have a customized plan for your session.

FREEDOM
IN CHRIST

STRONGHOLD-BUSTING

OBJECTIVE

To be equipped with a practical approach to replacing faulty beliefs with truth from God's Word so that we can make transformation a way of life.

LEADER'S NOTES

The first question in the Pause For Thought contains a list of common lies people believe and asks participants to find Bible verses that show what is really true. Here are some that we found:

Unloved: Jeremiah 31:3; John 3:16; 1 John 4:10

Rejected: John 1:12; Romans 8:1; 1 Corinthians 9:19–20; Ephesians 1:11; 1 Thessalonians 1:4

Inadequate: Jeremiah 1:6–7; John 15:16; 2 Corinthians 12:9, Philippians 4:13

Hopeless: Ephesians 1:10–13; 1 Thessalonians 5:18; 1 Timothy 4:10

Stupid: Romans 12:2; 1 Corinthians 1:26–29, 1 Corinthians 2:16, James 1:5

SMALL GROUP TIMINGS

The following plan is designed to help those leading the course in small groups. It assumes a meeting of around ninety minutes in length, and suggests how long each part of the session should last, with an indication of cumulative elapsed time. You will find a time plan in each session. The second column shows the time allocated to each individual element in minutes and seconds. The third column shows the total elapsed time in hours and minutes.

Stronghold-Busting Session	Minutes:Seconds	Hours:Minutes
Welcome, Focus, Connect	15:00	00:15
Word Part A	20:00	00:35
Pause For Thought 1	14:00	00:49
Word Part B	13:00	01:02
Reflect	28:00	01:30

The time allocated for the Word sections is based on the length of the corresponding section of the videos. Registered users of the course can download an Excel spreadsheet with these timings. Simply enter your own start time, adjust the length of the various components if desired and you will have a customized plan for your session.

FOCUS VERSE

Do not conform to the pattern of this world, but be transformed by the renewing of your mind. Then you will be able to test and approve what God's will is—his good, pleasing and perfect will.

Romans 12:2 NIV

FOCUS TRUTH

All of us have ingrained ways of thinking that are not in line with God's truth. Our success in continuing to walk in freedom and grow in maturity depends on the extent to which we renew our minds by uncovering these lies and replacing them with the truth from God's Word.

CONNECT

What is the best practical joke you have experienced?

When Jesus promises that we will know the truth and that the truth will set us free, He speaks as the One who also says that He *is* the Truth. What does it mean to you that Jesus actually *is* the Truth?

This is a very practical session designed to help people take personal responsibility to continue to walk in the freedom that they entered through *The Steps To Experiencing God's Grace*.

There are just two teaching sections, one Pause For Thought, and one Reflect. The reason we have shortened it is to enable you to spend significant time on the Reflect section in which participants will develop their first "Stronghold-Buster."

In our experience, those who really "get" the concept of stronghold-busting and make a commitment to do it, start to grow quickly as disciples, whereas those who don't tend not to.

It will be extremely useful if you can talk about stronghold-busting from personal experience. We encourage you to work one out for yourself and start it before you lead this session.

PRAYER & DECLARATION

In every session, we want to encourage people to pray out loud and to make a declaration out loud together. A prayer is addressed to God while a declaration is spoken out to the spiritual world in general.

Encourage people to make their declaration boldly!

Heavenly Father,

Thank You that the grace You showed us when Jesus went to the cross is available to us day by day. We pray today that You will guide us into all truth, reveal to us the strongholds in our minds, and help us to renew our minds, so that we will be transformed. We want to be disciples who bear much fruit. We choose to set our hope fully on the grace to be given to us when Jesus Christ is revealed.

In His name. Amen.

WE DECLARE THAT, EVEN THOUGH WE LIVE IN THE WORLD, WE DO NOT WAGE WAR AS THE WORLD DOES—WE FIGHT WITH WEAPONS WHICH HAVE DIVINE POWER! FOR EVERY UNHELPFUL WAY OF THINKING THAT HAS A "STRONG HOLD" ON US, WE CHOOSE TO BELIEVE GOD'S CLEAR PROMISE THAT WE CAN DEMOLISH THEM. NOT JUST COPE WITH THEM, WORK AROUND THEM, OR DO THEM A BIT OF DAMAGE. DEMOLISH THEM! AND IN SO DOING WE WILL BE TRANSFORMED BY THE RENEWING OF OUR MINDS.

WORD

PART A

WHAT ARE STRONGHOLDS?

Romans 12 (NIV) starts with, "I urge you, brothers and sisters, in view of God's mercy . . ." and then gives us two ways to respond to God's mercy.

The first is "to offer our bodies as a living sacrifice, holy and pleasing to God." We hope that you've taken that step and are choosing to stay put on the altar.

The second is "do not *conform* to the pattern of this world, but be *transformed* by the renewing of your mind."

This session is all about "stronghold-busting," a very practical way to renew your mind, that will help you experience the life transformation that God wants for you.

What do we mean by a "stronghold?"

The literal meaning of the word is a fortress, a strong defensive building. But on one occasion in the New Testament, Paul uses it as a metaphor. He says this:

For though we live in the world, we do not wage war as the world does. The weapons we fight with are not the weapons of the world. On the contrary, they have divine power to demolish strongholds. We demolish arguments and every pretension that sets itself up against the knowledge of God, and we take every thought captive to make it obedient to Christ. (2 Corinthians 10:3–5 NIV)

Who demolishes the strongholds? God? No, we do! Who takes every thought captive? We do.

Paul mentions *arguments* and *pretensions* that set themselves up against the true *knowledge* of God. He talks about taking every *thought* captive to make it obedient to Christ. The context is our mind, our thinking. And the word *stronghold* refers to a faulty belief that is deeply ingrained. It's been reinforced many times throughout your life and it's sitting there in your mind, strong and impenetrable—like a thick castle wall.

What makes this belief faulty, of course, is that it's not consistent with what God tells us is true in the Bible.

Where do these faulty beliefs come from?

Ephesians 2:2–3 says we all "followed the ways of this world and the ruler of the kingdom of the air, the spirit who is now at work in those who are disobedient. All of us lived among them . . . following its . . . thoughts" (NIV). Colossians 2:8 adds don't be held "captive by hollow and deceptive philosophy, . . . human tradition and the . . . spiritual forces of this world" (NIV).

Perhaps it started out back in childhood when a little thought was planted in your mind by something that happened to you—maybe you were bullied, or someone said something negative about you: "You're useless," "You're a failure," "You're ugly," "It's all your fault."

Later on the enemy lined up someone else who said or did the same thing. Since he knows your particular vulnerabilities, he ruthlessly exploits them by lining up people or circumstances one after the other to give you the same wrong message.

The world then adds insult to injury with its constant bombardment of lies about what it means to be successful or happy or loved.

And as it gets stronger and stronger, it becomes part of our default thinking and works itself out in our behavior. Then, whenever someone suggests we could go for a particular job or lead a small group at church, a voice plays in our mind: "I couldn't do that. I'm useless at that." We've believed it for so long it has become part of our lives, and we can't imagine it ever being any different.

Feelings of inferiority, insecurity, and inadequacy are all strongholds. Because no child of God is inferior, insecure, or inadequate.

Is any child of God dirty or ugly? Absolutely not. It isn't true. It just *feels* true. It's a lie that's been reinforced so many times that it literally gets a *strong hold* on you and causes you to think and act in ways that contradict God's Word.

It's like a Land Rover that drives through a muddy road the same way every day, making deep ruts that are then baked in the sun. Eventually you could take your hands off the steering wheel and it would follow the ruts. These ingrained thought patterns become our "default" ways of thinking and behaving.

Steering out of these ruts is possible, but it requires intentional effort.

Well, our actions always flow from our beliefs. Rotten beliefs and thoughts lead to bad actions, cross words, lousy choices . . . ultimately preventing us from experiencing the abundant life that God intends. A stronghold will always push us towards making bad choices because it is based on false information.

In Luke 6:45, Jesus said, "'For the mouth speaks what the heart is full of.'" If you don't like the words coming out of your mouth, if you're not pleased with the attitude you display, if you constantly criticize yourself—don't just try to change your outward behavior. Start with what's inside, the belief you hold that leads to the exterior fruit.

If you change the belief, your actions will follow. Perhaps you can see why this really does bring transformation.

For my first eight years of involvement with Freedom In Christ teaching, I failed to do even a single stronghold-buster. I didn't think I believed any lies! But three years ago, I made my first stronghold-buster. Do you want to hear it?

I reject the lie that I do not believe any lies. This lie stops me from growing closer to God. I accept the truth that my love for temporary worldly things shows that I do not yet love my Heavenly Father as I should. I invite the Spirit of Truth to guide me into all truth and show me the lies I believe.

As I declared that daily for forty days, the Holy Spirit gently revealed to me no fewer than seven lies that I believed. And that was just the beginning! Yes, it was humbling. He showed me these lies in three ways: One was as I argued against God's truth. As we were reading the new names in Christ, I got to the statement that said "my new name is pure," and I thought very sincerely "I want to be pure someday"—as if me being pure TODAY depended on my actions, not on what Christ had done for me . . . stronghold.

Reading through lists like "Who I am in Christ"—when you want to argue against one of them, thinking, that may be true of others but not of you; or even, you hope that can be true of you someday, but it's not today—this reveals a stronghold in your thinking.

Emotionally overreacting to simple situations also revealed to me that I had lies I believed about myself. Something that started as a small, insignificant issue brought out intense emotion and defensiveness on my part. Later I thought, "Why did I get so upset?" I realized I had a stronghold in there somewhere.

The third way God spoke into my life was through mature, grace-filled Christian friends. Friends point out strongholds to me. When they heard a lie revealed in my speech, they brought it to my attention. It's often easier to see the lie in someone else than to see it in yourself. After all, the lie you believe feels true to you.

PAUSE FOR THOUGHT 1

OBJECTIVE

To help people become clear about what a "lie" is and to start the process of determining what is actually true from God's Word.

1. When we talk about a "lie" on *The Grace Course*, we are referring to a belief that is not in line with what God says in His Word, the Bible. It may feel true but God says it is not true. Here is a list of common lies that people come to believe about themselves:

   Unloved

   Rejected

   Inadequate

   Hopeless

   Stupid

2. If you are comfortable to do so, share with the group a lie that you realize you have believed (it does not have to be on the list, of course).

3. For each lie that has been mentioned—or for the lies on the list—find a Bible verse to show that it is not true of any Christian.

PART B

DEMOLISHING STRONGHOLDS

They may have that strong hold on us, but God's clear promise is that we *can* demolish strongholds. Not just cope with them, work around them, or do them a bit of damage. Demolish them!

We're going to introduce you to "Stronghold-busting," but let's start with a bit of a health warning.

We see tremendous change in people's lives as they respond to God through our teaching. And it's amazing! But we also see people who seem to enjoy our courses for eight or ten weeks and learn some great stuff, however the impact gradually fades away because they don't make the effort required to change their thinking longer-term.

There are three factors to take into account:

First, this is your responsibility. Nobody else can renew your mind for you. And God won't do it either—in His wisdom and grace, it's something that He gives you the responsibility *and* ability to do. So, if you don't do it, it's not going to get done. And there'll be no lasting transformation.

Second, removing the footholds of the enemy that we've given him through sin by going through *The Steps To Freedom In Christ* or *The Steps To Experiencing God's Grace* can be done in a day. But busting a stronghold takes time, several weeks in fact. You will need to persevere—but it will be more than worth it.

Thirdly, by definition, the lies you believe *feel* absolutely true. They're not easy to recognize. It requires humility and intentionality to really bring your thoughts into the light of God's truth.

Because they might have been part of our thinking for such a long time, we think deep down that they can never be changed. And if you recognize that way of thinking in yourself, congratulations, you've just identified a stronghold that can be torn down!

It's very difficult to demolish a stronghold if you haven't first closed any doors in your life that are open to the enemy through unresolved sin.

Once you've done that, a mental stronghold is simply a habit that can be broken. And creating and using a "stronghold-buster" is a great way to break the habit.

STRONGHOLD-BUSTING

First, identify the faulty belief you want to change, the lie that you now realize is contrary to God's Word. This is what it means to "take captive every thought to make it obedient to Christ" (2 Corinthians 10:5 NIV). It means noticing what we are thinking, what we are saying, and considering whether it is in line with what God tells us is true.

Next, think about what effect believing that lie is having in your life. Realizing the negative effects will spur us on to tear the stronghold down.

Third, find the truth from God's Word that counteracts the lie. You can use a concordance, a Bible app, or a wise friend to help you find verses that speak truth opposing the lie you believe. Some people are tempted to find many verses. But often it's more effective to keep it simple, and focus on just a couple of verses that plainly put forward God's truth.

Let's give you an example of how this works. Your past experiences may have left you with a sense that you are helpless and that it would be hopeless to try to change. This has become a belief in your heart. If someone tries to tell you it's a lie, you even respond by thinking, "No, it's true." But turn to your Bible. What does it say?

Hebrews 13:5 says God will never leave you or forsake you. You can do all things through Him who gives you strength, Philippians 4:13. You are more than victorious through Jesus who loves you, Romans 8:37. Or take 2 Peter 1:3, which says God's divine power has given you everything you need for life and godliness. All truth from the Bible that contradicts that lie.

Next write a declaration:

"I refuse to believe the lie that I am hopeless and will never change.

"This lie has caused me to feel defeated and stopped me from overcoming sin in my life.

"I embrace the truth that God's divine power has given me everything I need for godliness and that I can do all things through Him who gives me strength. In Christ who loves me, I am more than victorious."

Then read the declaration out loud every day for forty days, all the time reminding yourself that, if God has said it, it really is true. The more you do it, the better. Morning and evening is great, but also "in the moment"—when you realize you're thinking or acting on that lie.

This is not as easy as it may sound because the lie behind the stronghold *feels* true to you.

As you go through your forty days, it's like a concrete wall being demolished. It withstands ten, twenty, thirty blows with no visible sign of being weakened. That's how it can feel as you work through a stronghold-buster day after day. In reality, tiny cracks are forming which are weakening the wall.

After thirty-seven swings there are still no signs of damage to the wall.

On the thirty-eighth swing—sooner or later—cracks become visible.

On the thirty-ninth swing, the cracks get bigger until finally the wall completely collapses. Your stronghold is broken down. Your mind—in that particular area—has been renewed.

Even though only the final three swings appear to have had an effect, without the previous thirty-seven, the wall would not have fallen.

Do persevere until you have completed at least forty days—or maybe even more—and remember that throughout most of that time it will feel like a complete waste of time, because the lie feels true to you. I promise you that if you persevere, you will tear the stronghold down. And you will be transformed.

We have mentioned that busting strongholds requires perseverance—that you need to stick with it for forty days, and that nobody can renew your mind for you. All of that is true, but don't walk away from this session thinking that it is by your own efforts that you will grow to serve God more faithfully. This is actually all about resting in His grace, accepting that what He said is indeed true. It's about taking Him at His word. And if you miss a day or two, God is not cross with you! Just pick up where you left off and keep going.

We have a couple of apps that include a Stronghold-Buster-Builder. This will remind you every day at a time of your choosing to make your declaration and bring it up on your screen. Details in your notes.

A word of advice—just do one stronghold-buster at a time. Tearing down strongholds is an endurance race, not a sprint. Once one has been demolished, then you can begin busting the next stronghold.

It's amazing when you experience that breakthrough.

When I realized that pride was keeping me living my life in my own strength, I recognized the consequence: I was getting anxious about what I was achieving, I'd get angry—especially with the kids when they disobeyed me. I realized I was basing my success as a father on the obedience of my children—and God said it's a good job He doesn't do that! John 5:30, Philippians 4:13, and John 15:16 helped bust the stronghold: Jesus said "I can do nothing on my own," but Paul said "I can do all things through Christ who strengthens me," and it is God who has appointed me to bear fruit in every situation. It's made a profound difference. Í m no longer striving as I used to. Rather than react to my kids in anger, I respond, seeing every challenge—well, okay, nearly every challenge—as an opportunity to demonstrate Goď s love, joy, peace, patience, kindness.

In conclusion, we want to leave you with 1 Peter 1:13 (NASB). "Prepare your minds for action." By renewing your mind, bringing it into alignment with God's truth—what He says about Himself and what He says about you—you will be much better equipped to serve God in this world and bear abundant fruit for His kingdom.

But again, it's not by our own efforts. The verse continues, ". . . set your hope on the grace to be brought to you when Jesus Christ is revealed" (NIV). The grace God showed us when Jesus went to the cross, and the grace He will show us when Jesus returns, is the same grace He shows us day by day to help us renew our minds and walk with Him in this world.

REFLECT

Introduction

1. Have you become aware of lies that you are prone to believe? What is the most significant one? Use this time to write a stronghold-buster.

2. First, identify the faulty belief you want to change, the lie that you now realize is contrary to God's Word.

3. Next, think about what effect believing that lie is having in your life.

4. Then find truth from God's Word that counteracts the lie.

5. Next write a declaration:

   "I refuse to believe the lie that . . . (whatever it is).

   This lie has caused (write down the effects in your life).

   I embrace the truth that . . .

6. Then write the numbers 1 through to 40 at the bottom and check one number off every day.

Reflection

7. Begin to create your very own stronghold-buster so that you can go on to demolish it. Use the guidelines in your Participant's Guide and take note of the sample stronghold-busters. You can also use the Stronghold-Buster Builder in our apps.

> CONCLUDING THE SESSION

Remind participants about "Daily Nuggets Of Grace," the devotional that accompanies this course that can be accessed on the YouVersion Bible App, *The Wonder Of Grace* introductory videos, and *The Grace Connection*, the book that accompanies *The Grace Course*.

Close in prayer.

> STRONGHOLD-BUSTING

> The weapons we fight with are not the weapons of the world. On the contrary, they have divine power to demolish strongholds. We demolish arguments and every pretension that sets itself up against the knowledge of God, and we take captive every thought to make it obedient to Christ. (2 Corinthians 10:4–5 NIV)

Ingrained habitual ways of thinking become deep ruts in our minds. The Bible calls them "strongholds." God's clear promise is that we can demolish them and be set free to think according to the truth. During *The Steps To Experiencing Grace,* you resolved the spiritual issues that the Holy Spirit revealed to you, and this will make it much easier to change ingrained ways of thinking than it was before.

Ongoing transformation will come only as you choose daily to renew your mind (Romans 12:2); that is to say, as you replace ingrained faulty beliefs with what God tells you in the Bible is actually true.

We strongly recommend that you ask God to show you one key belief that you now realize is false and use the following "Stronghold-Busting" process to demolish it over the coming weeks. Once you have replaced that lie with truth, do the same with another false belief, and then another as the Holy Spirit leads you.

1. IDENTIFY THE FAULTY BELIEF YOU WANT TO CHANGE.

That is what the Bible calls taking captive every thought to make it obedient to Christ. It means noticing what we are thinking and saying, and considering whether it is in line with what God tells us is true in His Word.

2. CONSIDER WHAT EFFECT BELIEVING THAT LIE IS HAVING IN YOUR LIFE.

Realizing the negative effects should spur us on to tear the stronghold down as we understand the positive changes that will bring.

3. MAKE A LIST OF KEY BIBLE VERSES THAT COUNTERACT THE LIE.

Your past experiences may, for example, have left you with a sense that you are helpless and that it would be hopeless to try to change. But God's Word makes some clear statements that contradict that: God will never leave you or forsake you (Isaiah 41:10–13, Hebrews 13:5–6); You can do all things through Jesus who gives you strength (Philippians 4:13).

4. WRITE A DECLARATION BASED ON THE VERSES.

Use the following pattern:

I refuse to believe the lie that . . . [eg.: I am dirty]

Believing this lie has . . . [eg.: given me a deep sense of shame, made me avoid people, etc.]

I embrace the truth that . . . [eg.: I have been washed clean by the blood of Jesus, that I am pure and holy, that I can draw near to God in full assurance, etc.]

5. READ THE DECLARATION OUT LOUD EVERY DAY FOR 40 DAYS.

The Bible says that "The tongue has the power of life and death" (Proverbs 18:21 NIV) and speaking out loud seems to help our minds take hold of the truth more effectively than simply reading silently.

Be warned! Stronghold-Busting is not as easy as it may sound because the lie behind the stronghold feels absolutely true to you. So, by definition, it will feel for some time as if you are wasting your time.

However, as you go through your forty days, it's like a concrete wall being demolished. It withstands ten, twenty, thirty blows of a sledgehammer with no visible sign of being weakened. As you work through it day after day, it will feel as if nothing is changing. However, eventually a few small cracks appear and then the cracks get bigger, and finally the wall completely collapses. Even though only the final few blows appear to have had an effect, without the previous blows, the wall would not have fallen. Persevere until the stronghold has been demolished and you really do know the truth that will set you free!

> STRONGHOLD-BUSTER EXAMPLE 1

FEAR OF DISAPPROVAL

The lie: I am unacceptable or just not good enough.

Effects in my life: feeling intimidated, fearing people, compromising my convictions, changing my appearance, anxious about saying and doing the "right thing"

The truth:

You did not choose me, but I chose you. (John 15:16)

[He] has also put his seal on us and given us his Spirit in our hearts as a guarantee. (2 Corinthians 1:22)

He will rejoice over you with gladness; he will quiet you by his love; he will exult over you with loud singing. (Zephaniah 3:17)

Man looks on the outward appearance, but the Lord looks on the heart. (1 Samuel 16:7)

The Lord is on my side; I will not fear. What can man do to me? (Psalm 118:6)

We have been approved by God to be entrusted with the gospel, so we speak, not to please man, but to please God who tests our hearts. (1 Thessalonians 2:4)

Dear Father God,

I refuse to believe the lie that I am not good enough or unacceptable.

Believing this lie has caused me to feel intimidated, to fear people, to compromise my convictions, to change my appearance, and to be over-anxious about saying and doing the "right thing."

I embrace the truth that You chose me and that I have received a new heart and therefore I have Your seal of approval. Even when others are not pleased with me, You take great delight in me and Your opinion matters much more.

I now choose to please You rather than other people and rely on Your promise to be with me wherever I go as I share the good news with others.

Amen.

1	2	3	4	5	6	7	8	9	10	11	12	13	14
15	16	17	18	19	20	21	22	23	24	25	26	27	28
29	30	31	32	33	34	35	36	37	38	39	40		

> STRONGHOLD-BUSTER EXAMPLE 2

FEAR OF FAILURE

The lie: When I fail I am worth less than before.

Effects in my life: being unwilling to attempt new challenges that are outside my comfort zone, being task-focused rather than people-focused, anger, competitiveness, striving for perfection

The truth:

You are precious in my eyes, and I love you. (Isaiah 43:4)

In [Christ] you have been made complete. (Colossians 2:10 NASB)

We are his workmanship, created in Christ Jesus for good works, which God prepared beforehand. (Ephesians 2:10)

[God] is able to do far more abundantly than all that we ask or think, according to the power at work within us. (Ephesians 3:20)

It is God who works in you, both to will and to work for his good pleasure. (Philippians 2:13)

Dear Heavenly Father,

I refuse to believe the lie that when I fail I am worth less than before.

Believing this lie has caused me not to attempt new things, to focus on tasks rather than people, to strive for perfection, and to feel angry and competitive.

I embrace the truth that I have been handcrafted by You and am precious, honored, and loved by You regardless of the success or failure of what I do. I declare that I am already fully complete in Christ and that You are working in me for Your good pleasure and to do far more abundantly than all I could ask or think.

In Jesus' name. Amen.

1	2	3	4	5	6	7	8	9	10	11	12	13	14
15	16	17	18	19	20	21	22	23	24	25	26	27	28
29	30	31	32	33	34	35	36	37	38	39	40		

> STRONGHOLD-BUSTER EXAMPLE 3

FEELING IRRESISTIBLY DRAWN TO PORN

The lie: I cannot resist the temptation to look at porn.

Effects in my life: deep sense of shame, warped sexual feelings, unable to relate to other people as God intended, harm to my marriage**The truth:**

In the same way, count yourselves dead to sin but alive to God in Christ Jesus. Therefore do not let sin reign in your mortal body so that you obey its evil desires. Do not offer any part of yourself to sin as an instrument of wickedness, but rather offer yourselves to God as those who have been brought from death to life; and offer every part of yourself to him as an instrument of righteousness. For sin shall no longer be your master, because you are not under the law, but under grace. (Romans 6:11–14 NIV)

Do you not know that your body is a temple of the Holy Spirit? (1 Corinthians 6:19)

No temptation has overtaken you except what is common to mankind. And God is faithful; he will not let you be tempted beyond what you can bear. But when you are tempted, he will also provide a way out so that you can endure it. (1 Corinthians 10:13 NIV)

So I say, walk by the Spirit, and you will not gratify the desires of the flesh. (Galatians 5:16 NIV)

But the fruit of the Spirit is love, joy, peace, patience, kindness, goodness, faithfulness, gentleness, self-control. (Galatians 5:22–23)

I refuse to believe the lie that I cannot resist the temptation to look at porn.

Believing this lie has given me a deep sense of shame, warped my sexual desires, prevented me from relating to other people as God intended, and harmed my relationship with my spouse.

I embrace the truth that God will always provide a way out when I am tempted, and I will choose to take it. I announce the truth that if I live by the Spirit—and I choose to do that—I will not gratify the desires of the flesh, and the fruit of the Spirit, including self-control, will grow in me. I count myself dead to sin and refuse to let sin reign in my body or be my master. Today and every day I give my body to God as a temple of the Holy Spirit to be used only for what honors Him.

I declare that the power of sin is broken in me. I choose to submit completely to God and resist the devil, who must flee from me now.

1	2	3	4	5	6	7	8	9	10	11	12	13	14
15	16	17	18	19	20	21	22	23	24	25	26	27	28
29	30	31	32	33	34	35	36	37	38	39	40		

RESOURCES

> CAN WE HELP YOUR CHURCH MAKE FRUITFUL DISCIPLES?

Most Christian leaders want to build communities that are healthy, growing, and full of life. So, it can be frustrating and discouraging when—despite trying everything—the reality falls short of the dream. We understand the discipleship journey can feel like hard work,

All too often, the problem is a culture of immaturity. If Christians in a community lack the desire or direction to take ownership of their spiritual growth, then it's hard to achieve any meaningful momentum.

Freedom In Christ's discipleship resources give church leaders and their churches a proven roadmap to spiritual maturity that makes discipleship a joy, not a burden, and empowers people to disciple others.

As a result, leaders gain renewed energy in their calling as they grow flourishing communities of life-long disciples, fulfill God's purposes, and make a difference in the world.

OUR DISCIPLESHIP APPROACH

We eschew "try harder" or "behave better" messages and replace them with simple, powerful, biblical principles for life that anyone, anywhere, anytime can use and pass on to others.

TRUTH: Come to know the incredible love of God in your heart, not just your head; know just who you now are in Christ; understand the nature of the spiritual battle and the resources you have in Christ to stand firm.

TURNING: Understand and practice repentance so that you ruthlessly close any doors you've opened to the enemy through past sin and don't open any more.

TRANSFORMATION: Learn practically how to renew your mind by replacing faulty beliefs that have developed with the truth from God's Word.

A LONG-TERM WHOLE-CHURCH STRATEGY

Our discipleship resources provide a proven roadmap to spiritual maturity that releases disciples to make disciples.

We have testimonies from thousands of Christian leaders who have achieved transformational results with Freedom In Christ.

We do not offer a "one size fits all" approach but love to help each church team identify their specific calling and gifting and select the tools that are appropriate for their own situation.

We provide a self-guided process that's clearly explained and, in many countries, a network of local people who can "train your trainers" and support you every step of the way. Our discipleship approach is infinitely transferable. Anyone can learn these principles and use them to grow and disciple others. This means that you can quickly and easily build a team to transform discipleship in your church.

We have a particular heart—and highly effective programs—to equip leaders personally.

THE DISCIPLESHIP HUB—ALL OUR RESOURCES TOGETHER IN ONE PLACE

Designed specifically for church and small group leaders, this online platform houses all of Freedom In Christ's material and offers a seamless and user-friendly experience.

It includes not just the videos but access to the accompanying notes, all in an easy-to-use format.

Use it to run small groups—there are tools for interaction, monitoring activity, and communication—or to give individuals access to the courses.

TAKING IT FORWARD

New to Freedom In Christ? Try it for yourself by taking the Freedom In Christ Course or joining our ten-month *Transform* program for leaders.

Looking for more? Choose from our library of courses for you, your team, or your church.

Join our Leaders Community on social media.

> **To get in touch with Freedom In Christ Ministries in your country and for further information and help, please go to**
> www.FreedomInChrist.org/leaders

COURSES DESIGNED BY CHRISTIAN LEADERS FOR CHRISTIAN LEADERS

>TRANSFORM

A PERSONAL JOURNEY FOR CHRISTIAN LEADERS INTO GREATER FREEDOM, FRUITFULNESS, AND DISCIPLE-MAKING.

"TRANSFORM succeeded in mending gaps in my spiritual life and repositioned me for the various tasks ahead of me. I would highly recommend it to any leader."

"I would strongly recommend it to any Christian in a leadership position, whether it's in church, ministry, public service, or business. It's a wonderful opportunity for personal growth in intimacy with God, in a safe setting, with excellent input and fellowship—something I've rarely found as a leader."

"God uses different tools to sharpen us. TRANSFORM is one of those tools. It's a journey where you dive into truths and are deeply challenged to be more like Jesus."

TRANSFORM is specifically designed for church leaders and leaders of Christian organizations who are passionate about leading a church or ministry of fruitful disciples that makes a major impact for the Kingdom of God.

It will help you ground your leadership firmly in the biblical principles of identity, freedom, and transformation, and equip you to go even deeper into God personally, confident that this will lead to greater influence and fruitfulness in your life and ministry. You will then be well placed to kick-start or accelerate the process of personal and corporate discipleship in your church.

TRANSFORM is a nine-month program of weekly study, reflection, and fellowship run online by Freedom In Christ using Zoom conferencing and two retreats. Guided and directed by a dedicated Transform leader, you will go through three stages—*Reposition*, *Retune,* and *Refocus* - with a "community" of like-minded leaders all traveling through the Transform journey. There will be an abundance of sharing, discussion, and prayer throughout the process.

> FREED TO LEAD

"It has reinforced my conviction that my identity is first and foremost in Christ, whatever leadership role I may hold."

"The Freed To Lead course has been the most amazing leadership development experience of my career, having been called to both marketplace and church leadership for over twenty years. It dispels worldly leadership myths and practices and provides biblical foundations for Godly leadership. I wholeheartedly recommend this course for anyone who aspires or is currently called to Godly, servant-hearted leadership in any arena."

"An outstanding course—inspirational and motivational, affirming and encouraging."

At a time of complex leadership challenges in churches, where Christian leaders face huge obstacles and struggle to balance corporate and Christian leadership styles, *Freed To Lead* will help you lead out of your identity in Christ.

It's a powerful 10-week video-led discipleship course for Christians who are called to leadership—whether in the marketplace, public service, the Church or any other context. *Freed to Lead* shows how being rooted in Christ is the true foundation for all Christians with responsibility for leading or managing others.

Written by Christian leaders for Christian leaders, it will transform your approach to leadership, free you from drivenness and burnout, enable you to survive personal attacks, use conflict positively, and overcome other barriers to effective leadership.

Freed to Lead will help you discover how to develop a healthy approach to leadership and stay on course to achieve your God-given vision.

Church leadership teams will benefit hugely from going through it together before rolling it out to others in their church who are in leadership in any sphere or think they may be called to leadership in the future.

Ten–session course or retreat plus *The Steps to Freedom For Leaders*

- A dedicated *Freed To Lead* book by Christian author and church leader, Rod Woods

- An excellent follow–up to *The Freedom In Christ Course* and *The Grace Course*

- Video testimonies and "Pause For Thought" discussion times.

DISCIPLESHIP COURSES FOR ALL

> THE FREEDOM IN CHRIST COURSE

"Men, women, and middle and high school students have been radically transformed."

Bob Huisman, Pastor, Immanuel Christian Reformed Church, Hudsonville, MI, USA

"I recommend it highly to anyone serious about discipleship."

Chuah Seong Peng, Senior Pastor, Holy Light Presbyterian Church, Johor Baru, Malaysia

"The Freedom In Christ Course changed me and put me in a position to minister to people in a much more effective way."

Frikkie Elstadt, Every Nation Patria, Mossel Bay, South Africa

"Our church has changed as a result of this course. Those who come to Christ and who do the course end up with a rock solid start to their faith."

Pastor Sam Scott, Eltham Baptist Church, Australia

Now in its third edition and translated into well over forty languages, *The Freedom In Christ Course* can transform the way you help Christians become fruitful disciples. It is our main discipleship resource and versions are available for different ages so that you can run the same teaching right across the ages at the same time. Focused on firstly establishing every Christian in the sure foundation of their identity in Jesus, it gives them the tools to break free and stay free from all that holds them back, and a strategy for ongoing transformation.

It has ten teaching sessions presented by Steve Goss, Nancy Maldonado, and Daryl Fitzgerald plus *The Steps To Freedom In Christ* ministry component presented by Steve Goss and Neil Anderson.

Unique to Freedom In Christ, *The Steps to Freedom In Christ*, is a powerful, step-by-step prayer repentance process that enables participants to resolve their personal and spiritual conflicts by submitting to God and resisting the devil, thereby experiencing their freedom in Christ (James 4:7). It is a gentle and straightforward process just between the participant and God, during which participants uncover "strongholds" that they have developed in their thinking that can be addressed through renewing their mind.

With a specially designed app, extra teaching films, a worship album, a Leader's Guide, a Participant's Guide, and tons of extras, *The Freedom In Christ* course offers you everything you need to make disciples who bear fruit that will last!

> KEYS TO HEALTH, WHOLENESS, & FRUITFULNESS

"It has given me such freedom to realize that my identity is not tied to any disease, and I don't have to 'own' it."

"I've had some issues about feeling worthless because of what people have said in my past. I looked at the Scriptures and found out who I really am in Christ. That's just really transformed me!"

"This course has made me realize how God heals not only spiritually but through my doctor as well."

"We're surrounded by 'good advice' about health, and you never really know what to believe. A true understanding of wholeness came through from both the medical and the spiritual sense."

Keys To Health, Wholeness, & Fruitfulness is a video-based discipleship course for every Christian. Written and presented by Steve Goss, Dr. Mary Wren, and Dr. Ifeoma Monye, it brings together truth from the Bible and wisdom from the medical world to equip you to be a healthy, whole disciple of Jesus whose life really counts.

The objective of the course is to understand that good physical health is not an end in itself, but a means to help us be and do all that God intends for us as fruitful disciples of Jesus. A complete answer comes only by considering the whole person, spirit, mind, and body.

Dr. Mary Wren, co-author of this course, is a practicing medical doctor. As a student, she had serious illnesses during which she started to learn how to seek God for help and wisdom, as well as seeking medical help. She sees herself as a bridge between medicine and the Church.

- Understand how to look after your whole being—spirit, mind, and body.
- Uncover the roots of health issues and learn to resolve them.
- Live well despite the limitations of your physical body.
- Get rid of stress, anxiety, and fear.
- Learn how to make consistent, healthy choices.
- Deal with negative habits that try to control you.
- Understand what the Bible teaches about healing.
- Discover why physical death holds no fear.

The course includes an eight-point plan to ensure you've done everything you're responsible to do for healing, and the *Steps to Healing & Wholeness.*

DEDICATED COURSES FOR YOUNGER GENERATIONS

We understand discipling the next generation requires a different approach. At Freedom In Christ, we have developed bespoke courses that address different age cohorts with a number of courses dedicated to their specific age group and needs.

Our courses range from a course for those in their 20s and 30s, a new course for 11- to 18-year-olds, and a course written specifically by children's ministers for 5- to 11-year-olds.

> THE LIGHTBRINGERS

ACTION-PACKED RESOURCE WITH TEN TEACHING SESSIONS FOR CHILDREN AGED 5 TO 11 IN TWO AGE GROUPS (5–8 AND 9–11).

The Lightbringers is a fantastic resource to help children understand their identity in Christ and show them how to view the rest of the world through that lens. It helps children come to know who they are in Jesus and equips them as they grow into young adults.

An interactive and immersive course, videos with action-packed stories bring biblical truth to life through "The Adventures of Lily Pepper" for 5–7s and "The Lightbringers" for 8–11s. There are also specially written praise and worship songs for each session.

The course incorporates all three "Ts" of the Freedom In Christ approach, including an interactive children's version of *The Steps To Freedom In Christ* called *The Lightbringers Trail*.

Written by Mark Griffiths and Joanne Foster, both specialists in children's ministry, it is designed to equip children to become fruitful disciples and stay connected with Jesus into their adult lives.

The Church Edition contains everything a church needs: a comprehensive hard copy Leader's Guide and online access to downloadable videos, songs, activity sheets, and PowerPoint presentations. Use it with as many children as you like for as long as you like without paying any more.

The Family Edition is a slimmed-down version designed for use on a tablet by parents at home.

> iGEN

FREEDOM IN CHRIST FOR YOUNG PEOPLE AGED 11 TO 18.

Reaching today's youth with the gospel of Jesus Christ and the message of Freedom In Christ is vital, and spreading the gospel is not just an older generation to younger generation plan.

iGEN is a discipleship resource designed to set young believers free to reach their generation with the good news of Jesus and the message of identity-based discipleship.

It is designed to draw out participant conversation in spaces that are safe, unpressured, and non-judgmental. Participants will have opportunities to ask questions, express faith or doubts, and share their personal struggles and victories. Live interaction combined with clearly communicated truth will produce positive spiritual impact.

Hosted exclusively on our Discipleship Hub platform, iGen consists of:

- Ten sessions based on *The Freedom in Christ Course*

- A youth version of *The Steps to Freedom in Christ*Accessed online via devicesVideo presented by an international cast of excellent communicators

- Each iGen session has embedded breaks for group interaction and discussions

iGEN works in a variety of youth contexts. The Leader's Guide will help you to adapt it to your specific needs.

A version in Spanish is also available.

> DISCIPLE

FOR 20S AND 30S

"You really get us and understand us; you don't just patronize us and talk down to us."

"God is doing incredible things in the young people at our church, and I'm just grateful this course has been able to facilitate that."

"Thank you so much for caring enough to do this. You have no idea how much it means to us that you have taken the time to understand and help us overcome all the stuff that comes at us."

"Disciple is so user-friendly. The young adults really engaged, and there were definite lightbulb moments. The Freedom In Christ message really comes across, but in a different way to the Freedom In Christ Course. It's been three months since we did it, and everyone still refers to it."

Church leaders report that discipling those in their 20s and 30s is one of their biggest challenges. *Disciple* is a powerful tool to help you. It speaks the language of the 20s and 30s and invites them to dive into the greatest story ever told, God's story. They will learn how to take hold of their freedom and discover their mandate from God.

- Ten sessions designed to run for approximately 90 minutes each

- Impactful Starter Films introduce the theme for each session

- Extra films (via the app) on topics including Sex, the Occult, and Fear

- Chat and Reflect times allow teaching to take root

- App with extra teaching films, daily devotional, daily nuggets of extra teaching, and Stronghold–Buster Builder with reminders

FREEDOM IN CHRIST

BECOME A FRIEND OF FREEDOM IN CHRIST

Freedom In Christ Ministries was founded over 30 years ago by Dr. Neil T Anderson. We offer a unique approach to discipleship based on our three core principles of Truth, Turning, and Transformation.

Now based in 40 countries with translations in over 30 languages, Freedom In Christ has equipped millions of Christians worldwide to cultivate a lifestyle of unstoppable spiritual growth.

WILL YOU STAND WITH US?

Have you seen people's lives transformed through this course? Would you like to be involved in making the impact even greater? If you are excited about the effect this teaching can have on individuals, churches, and communities, we'd love to have you on the team!

JOIN OUR TEAM OF INTERNATIONAL SUPPORTERS

Freedom In Christ exists to equip the Church worldwide to make fruitful disciples. We rely heavily for financial support on people who have understood how important it is to give leaders the tools that will enable them to help people become fruitful disciples, not just converts,

especially when we are opening up an office in a new country.

Typically your support will be used to:

- help us equip church leaders around the world
- open Freedom In Christ offices in new countries
- translate our discipleship resources into other languages
- develop new discipleship resources

JOIN THE TEAM OF SUPPORTERS IN YOUR COUNTRY

We are passionate about working with those who have themselves been touched by the biblical message of freedom. Financial support enables us to develop new resources and get them into the hands of more church leaders. As a result many, many people are connecting with this life-changing message. There are always new projects—small and large—that don't happen unless there's funding for them.

To find out more about partnering with us please go to: FreedomInChrist.org/friends